Coloring Book For Adults
Mandala Vision

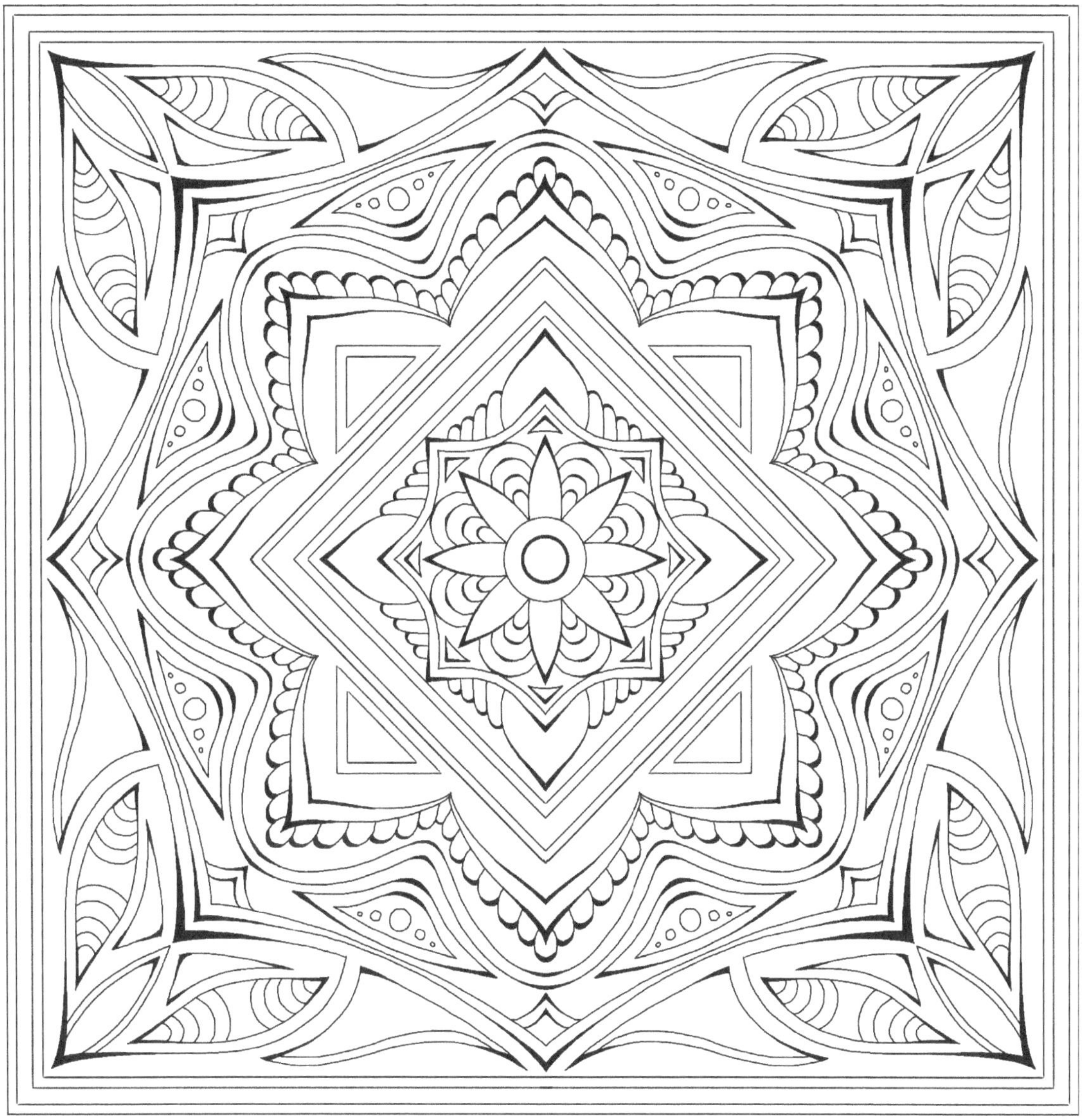

© Lexa Wagner

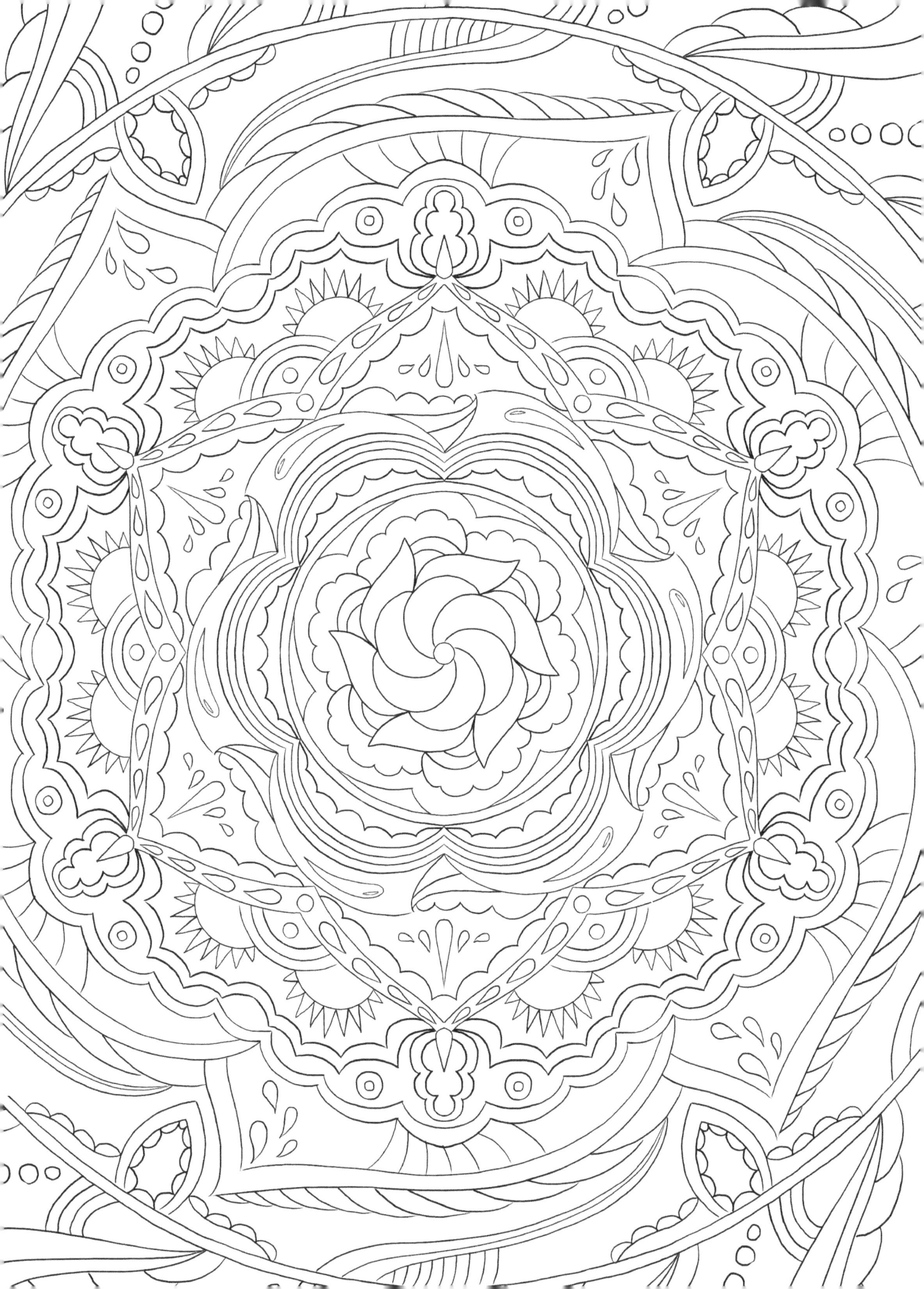

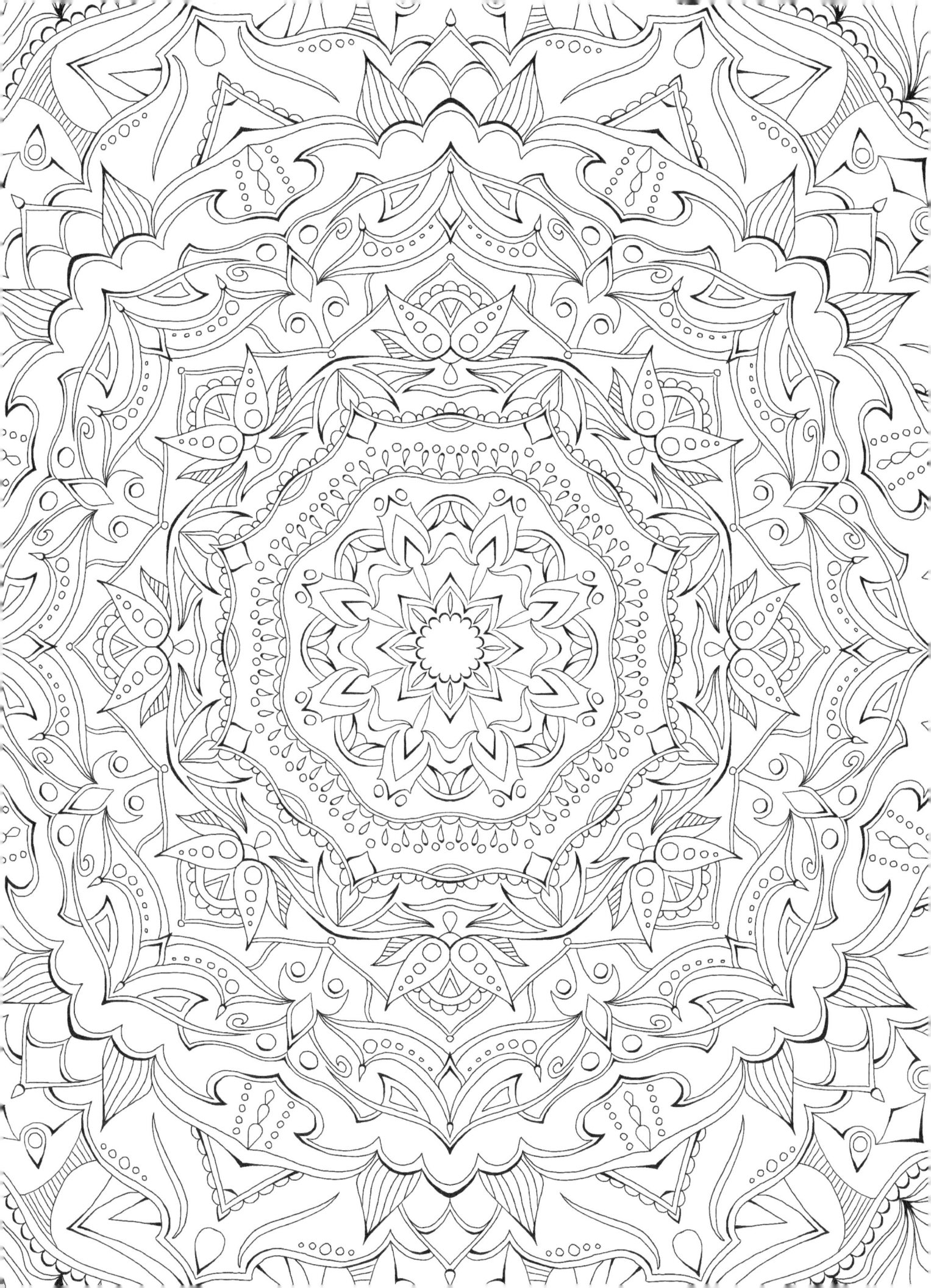

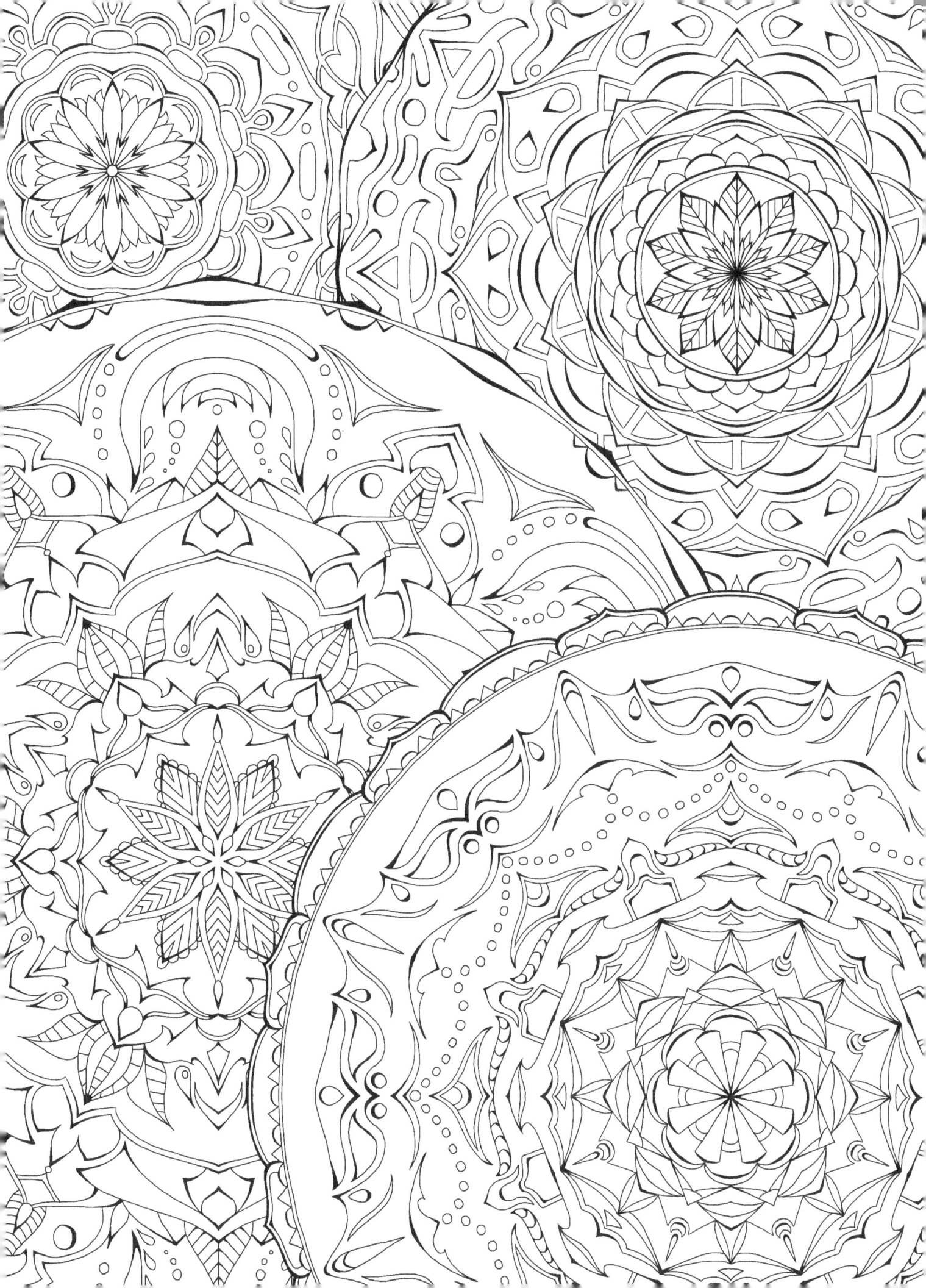

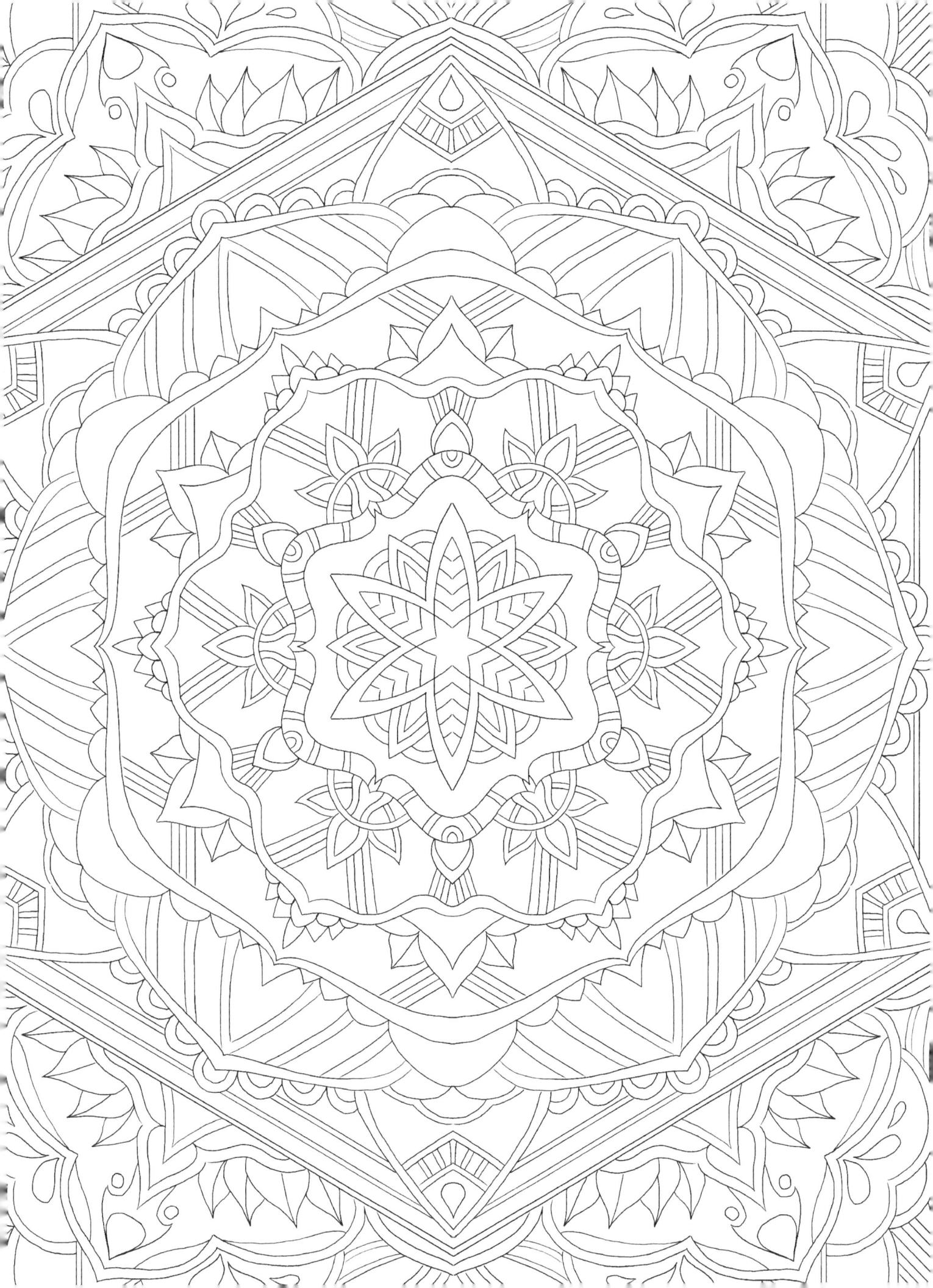

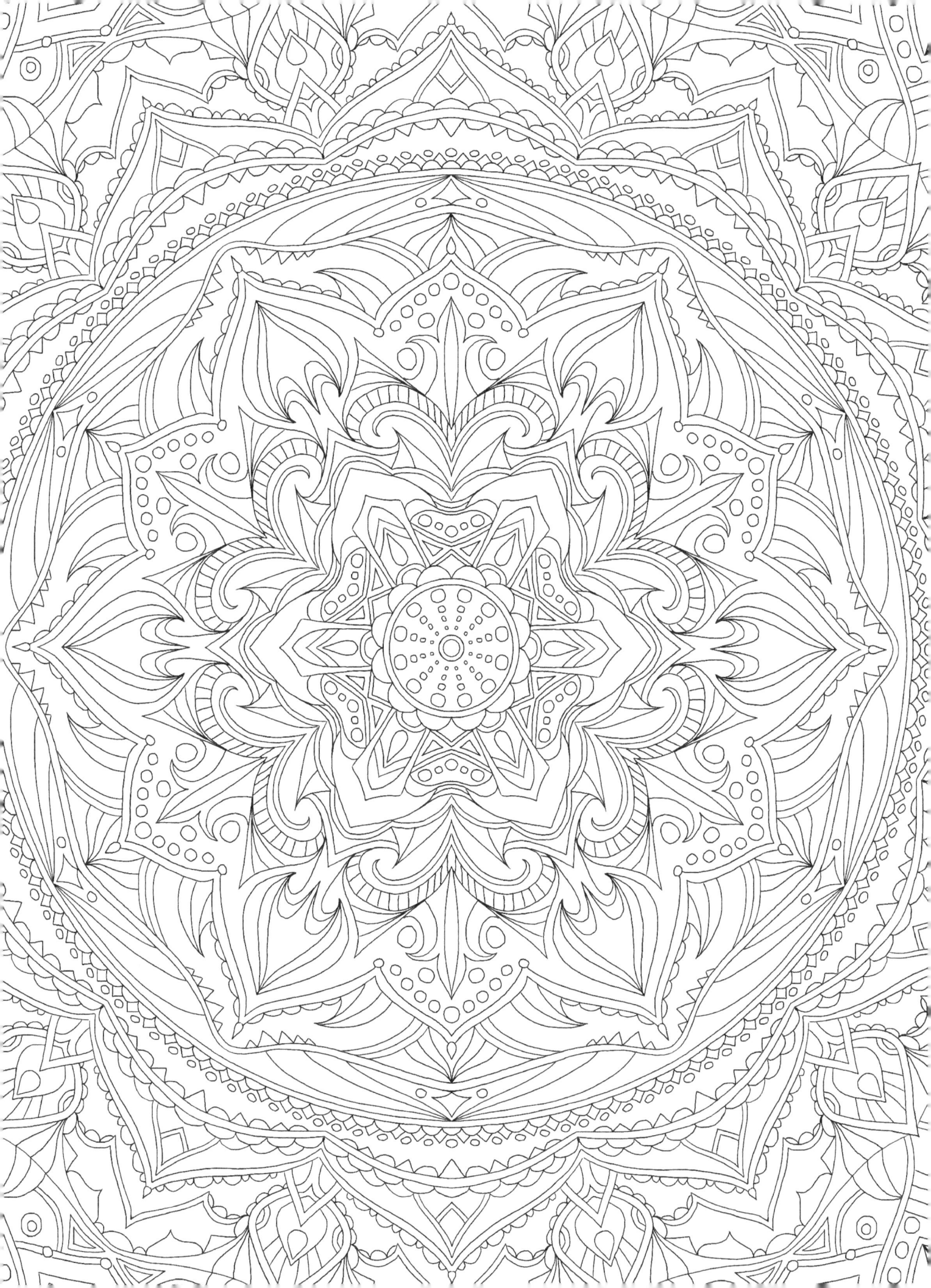

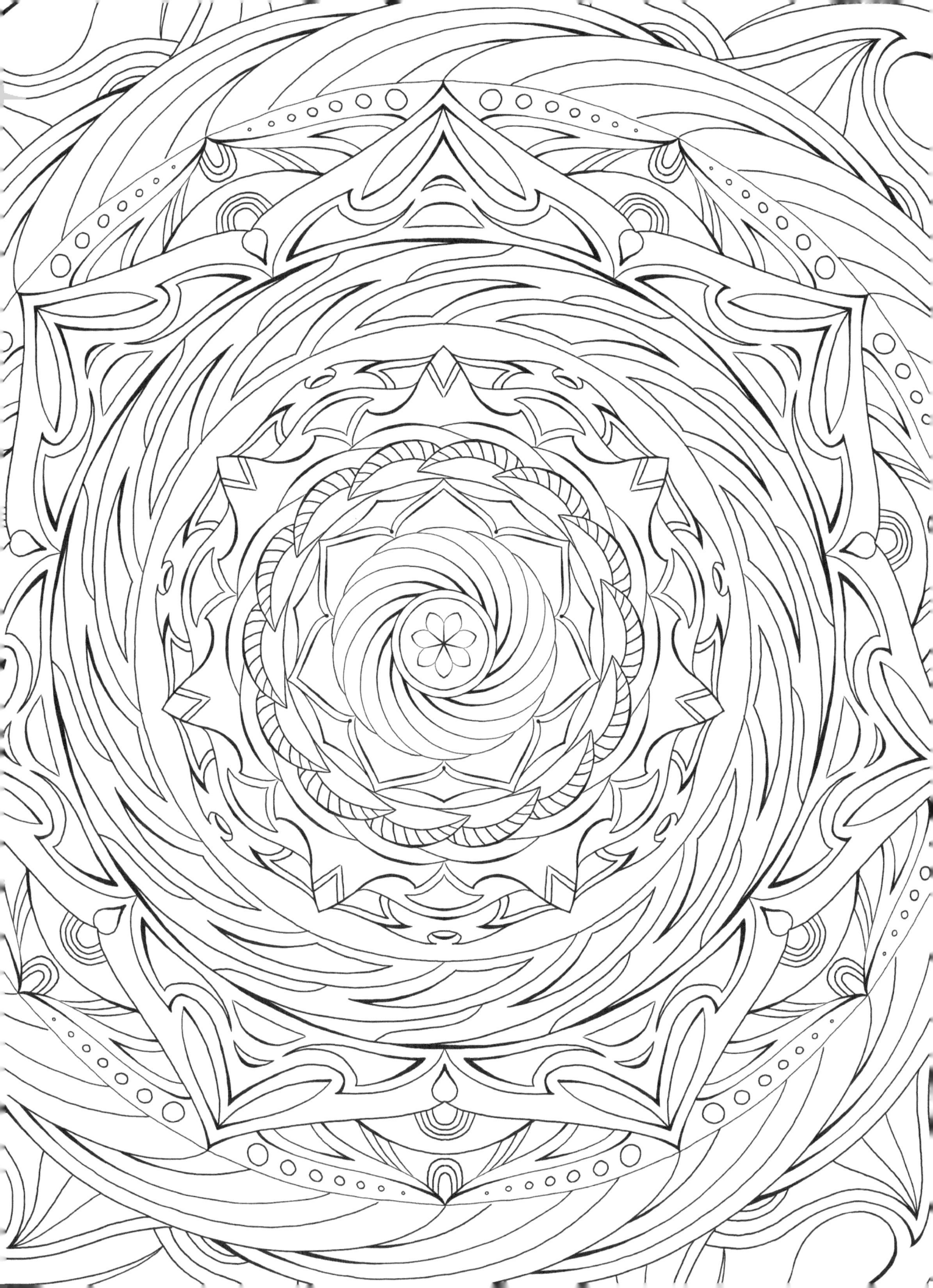

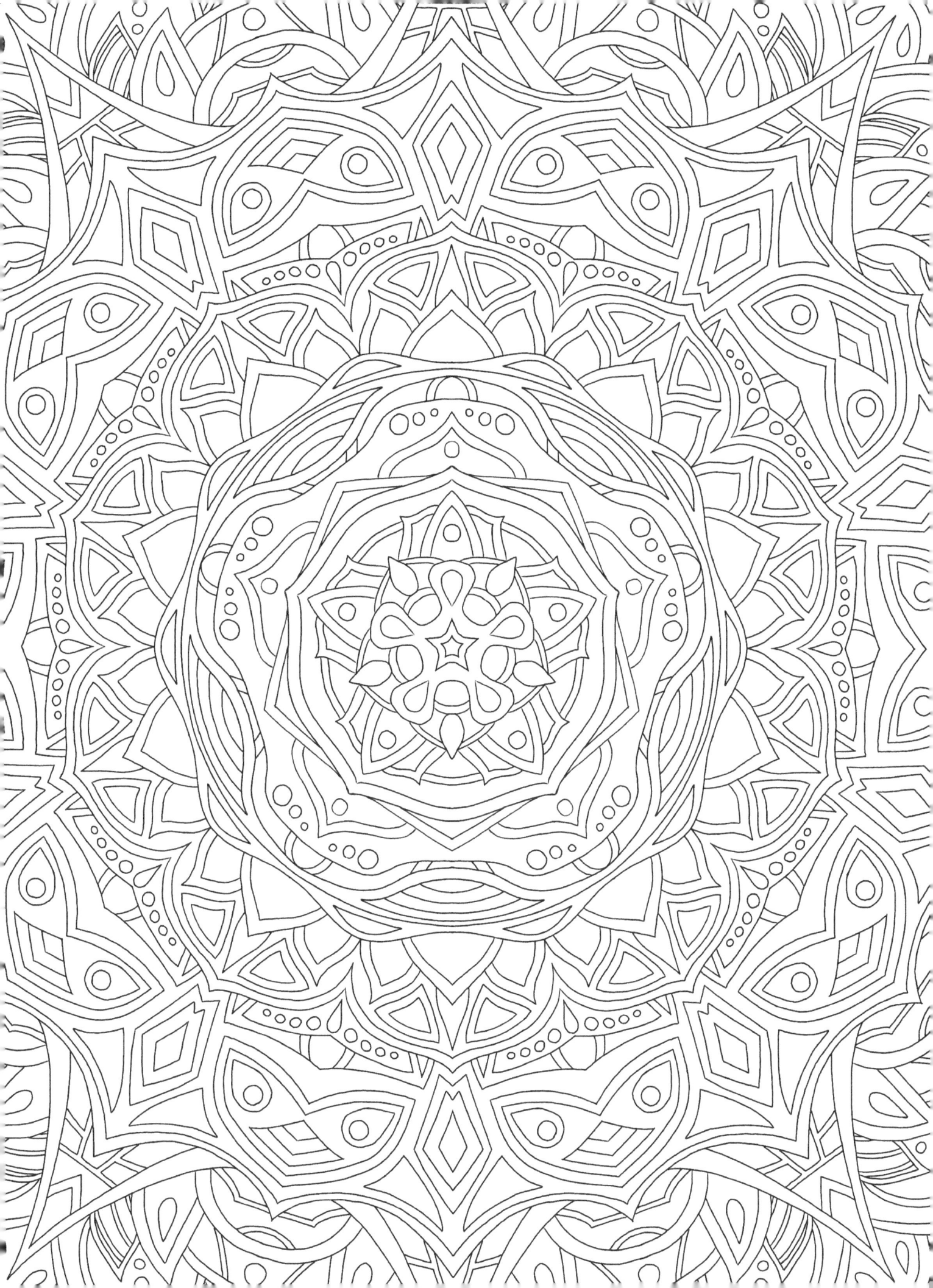

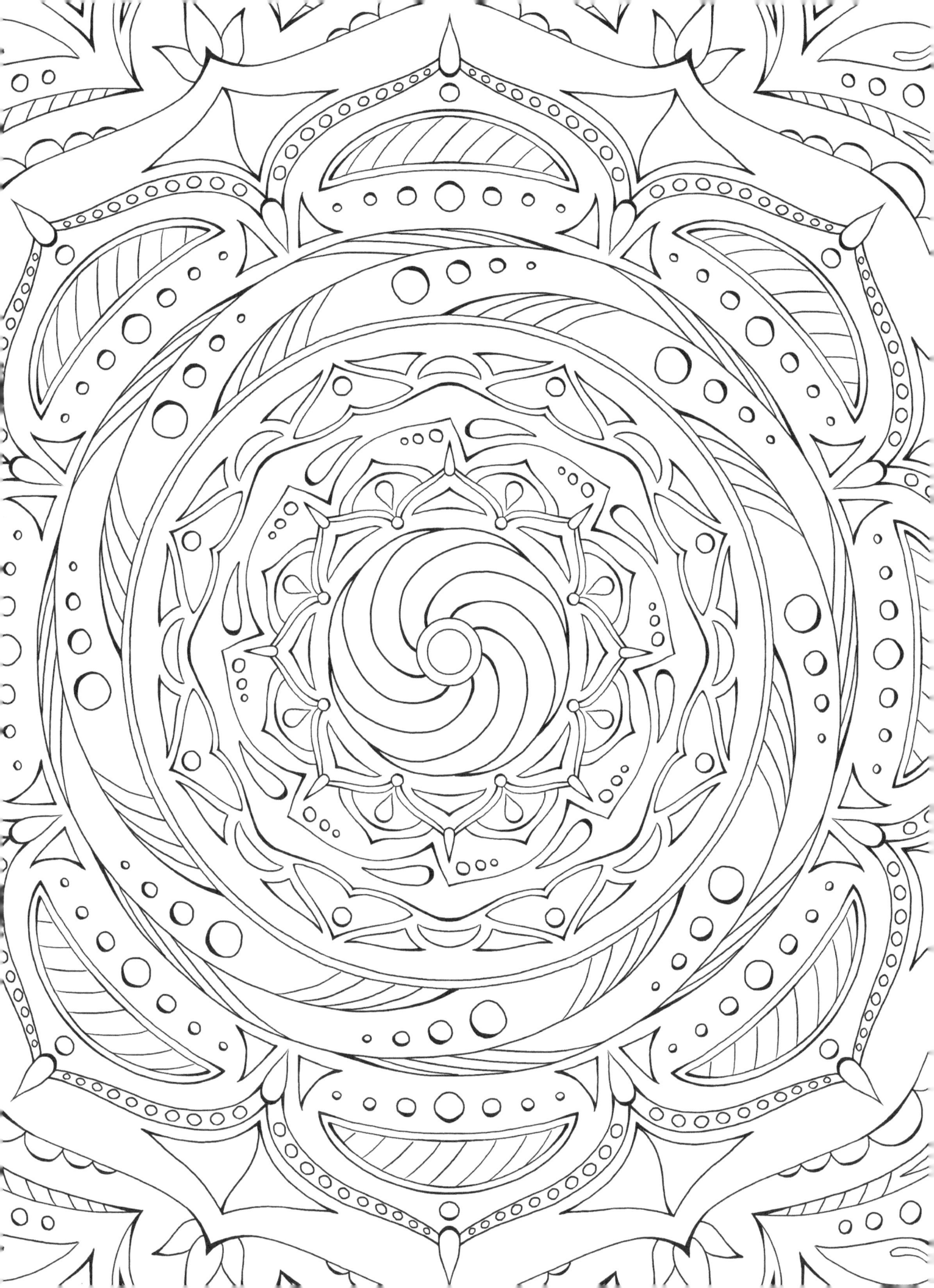

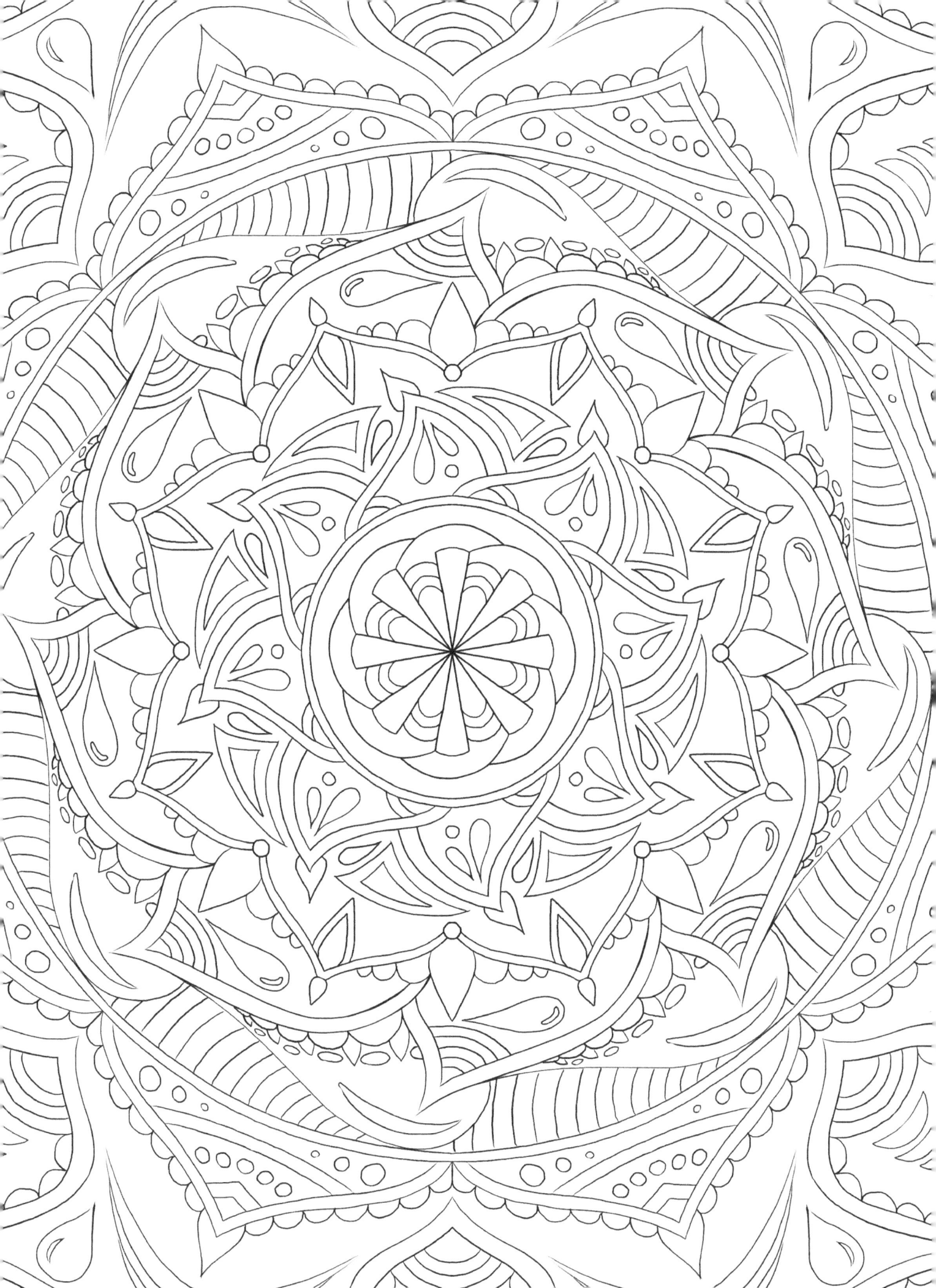

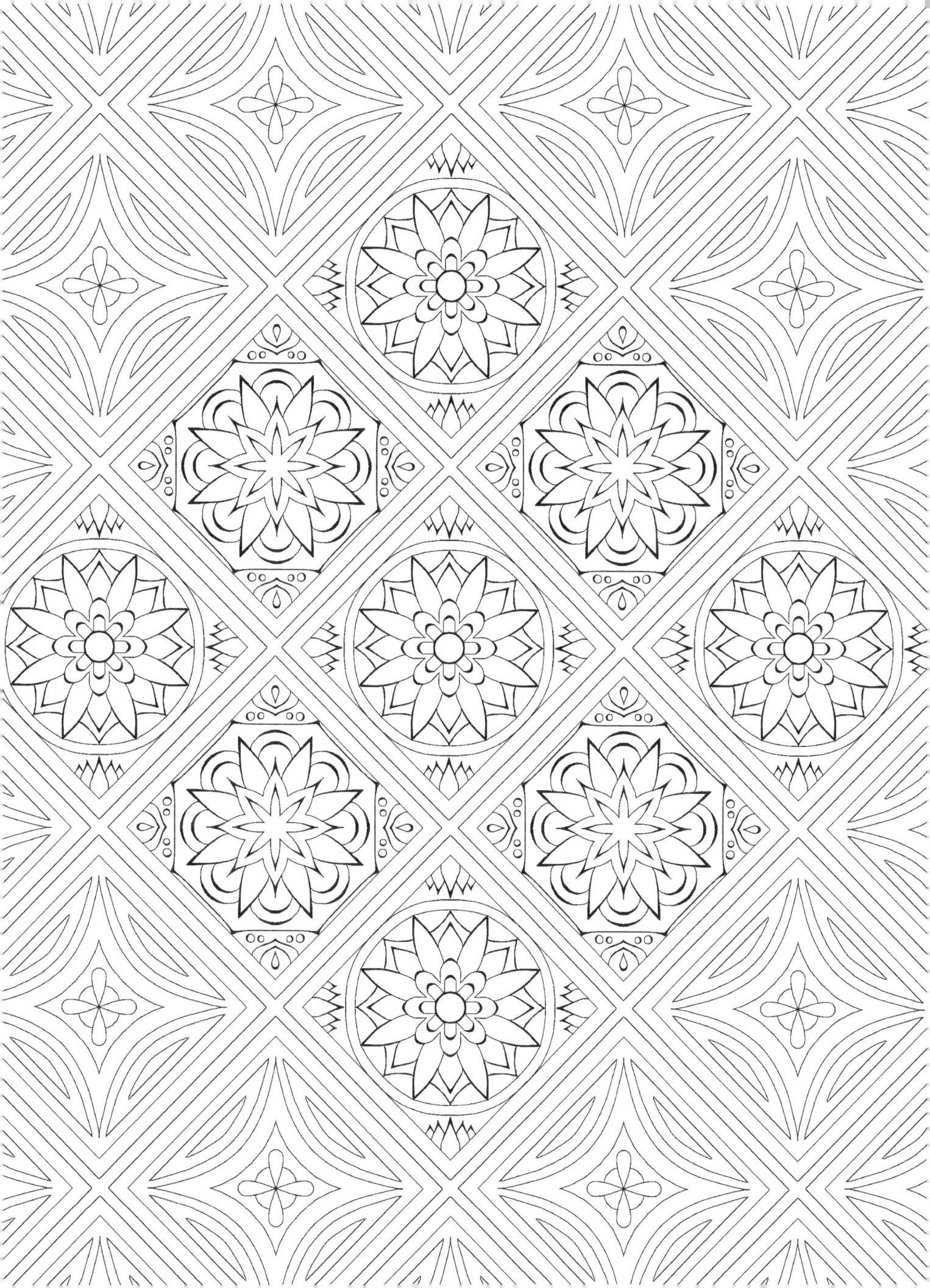

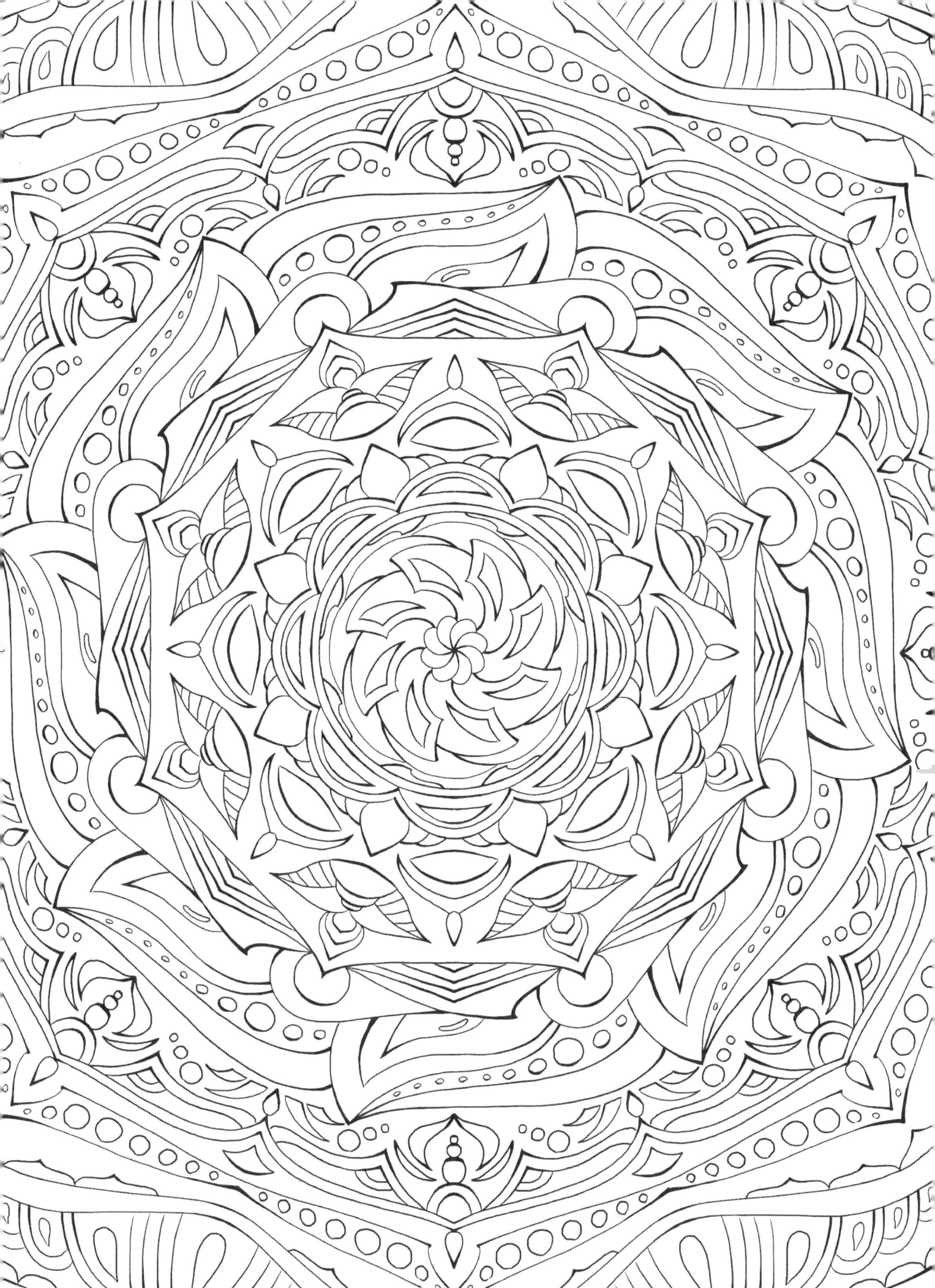

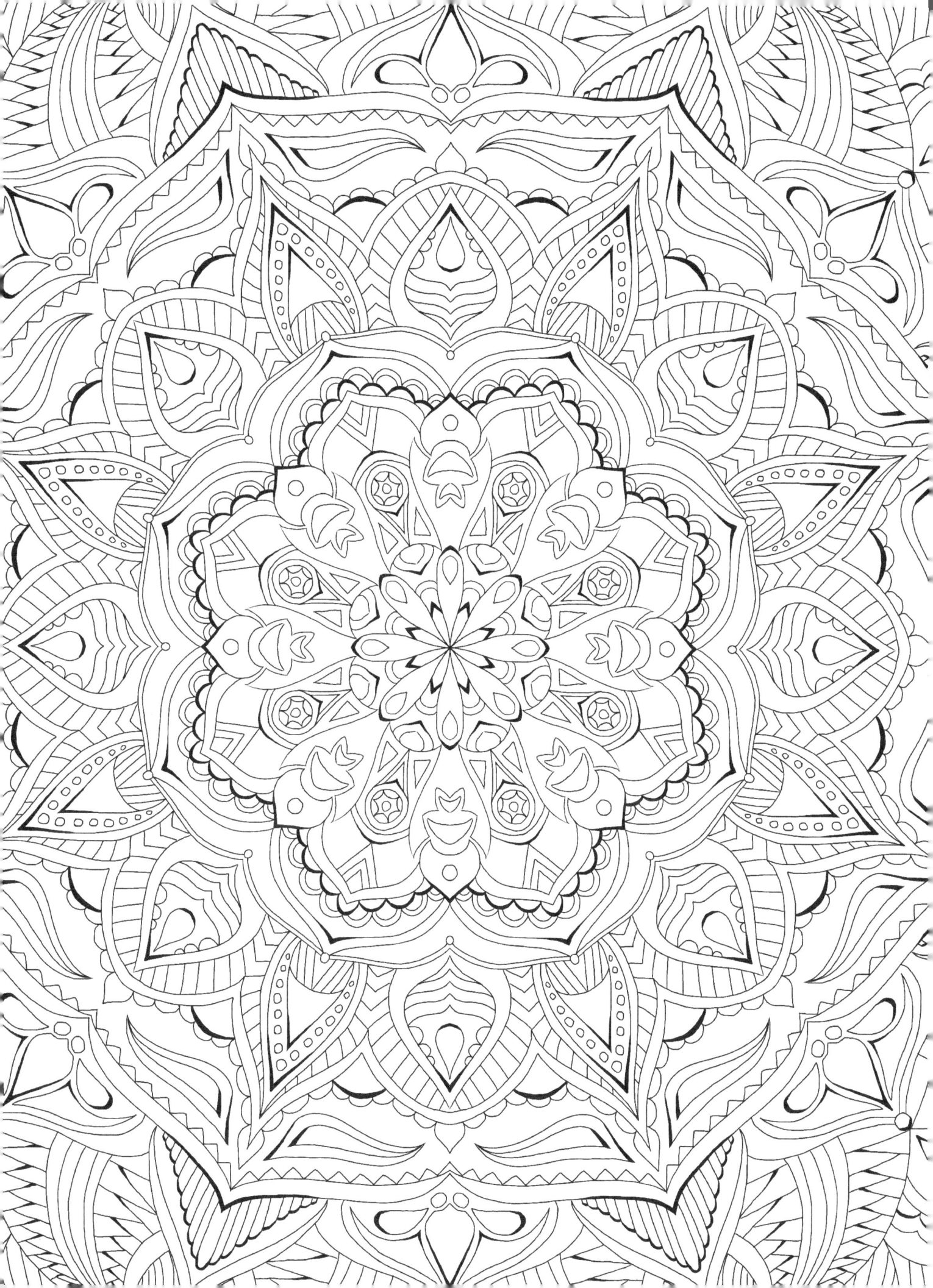

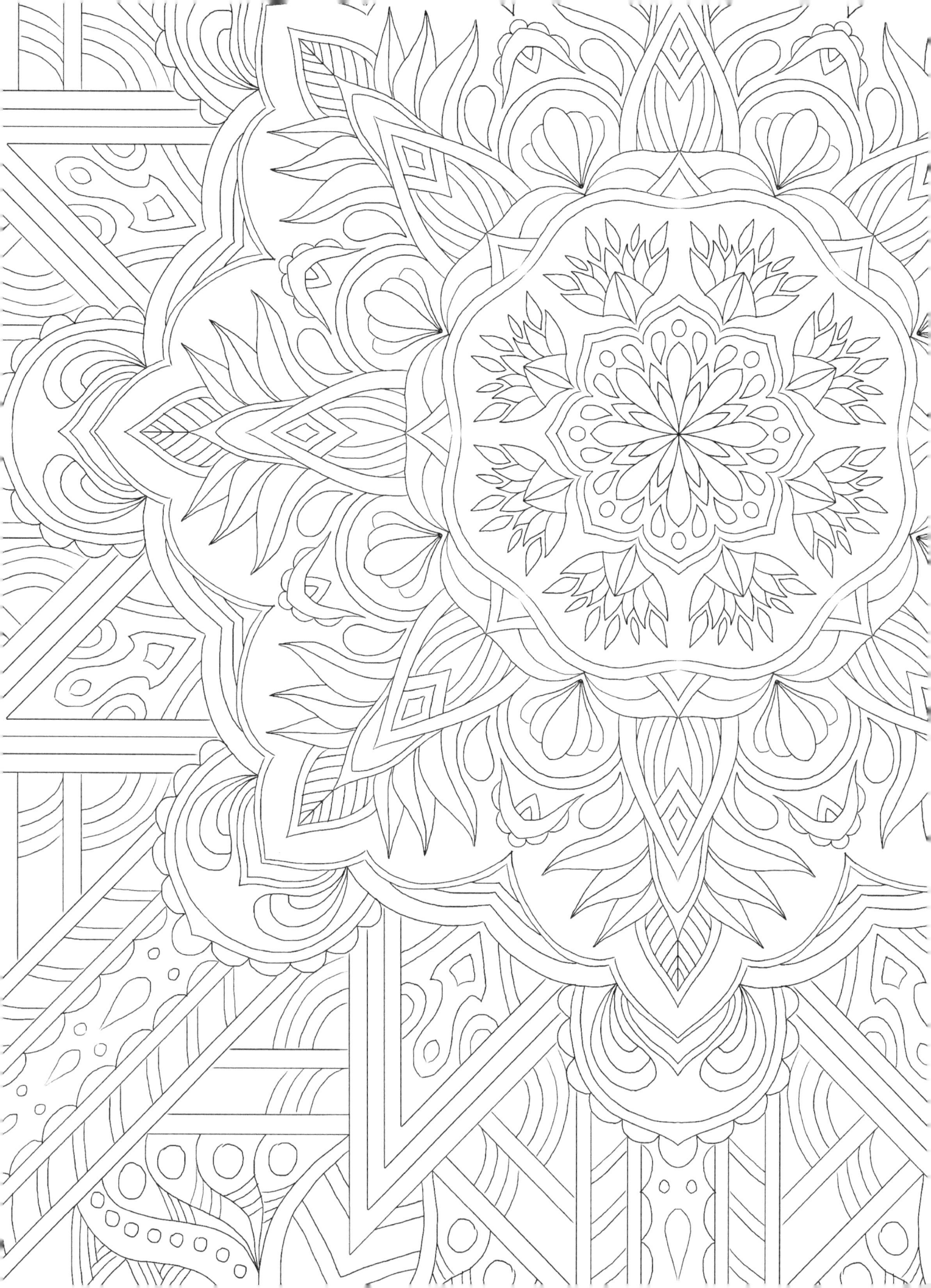

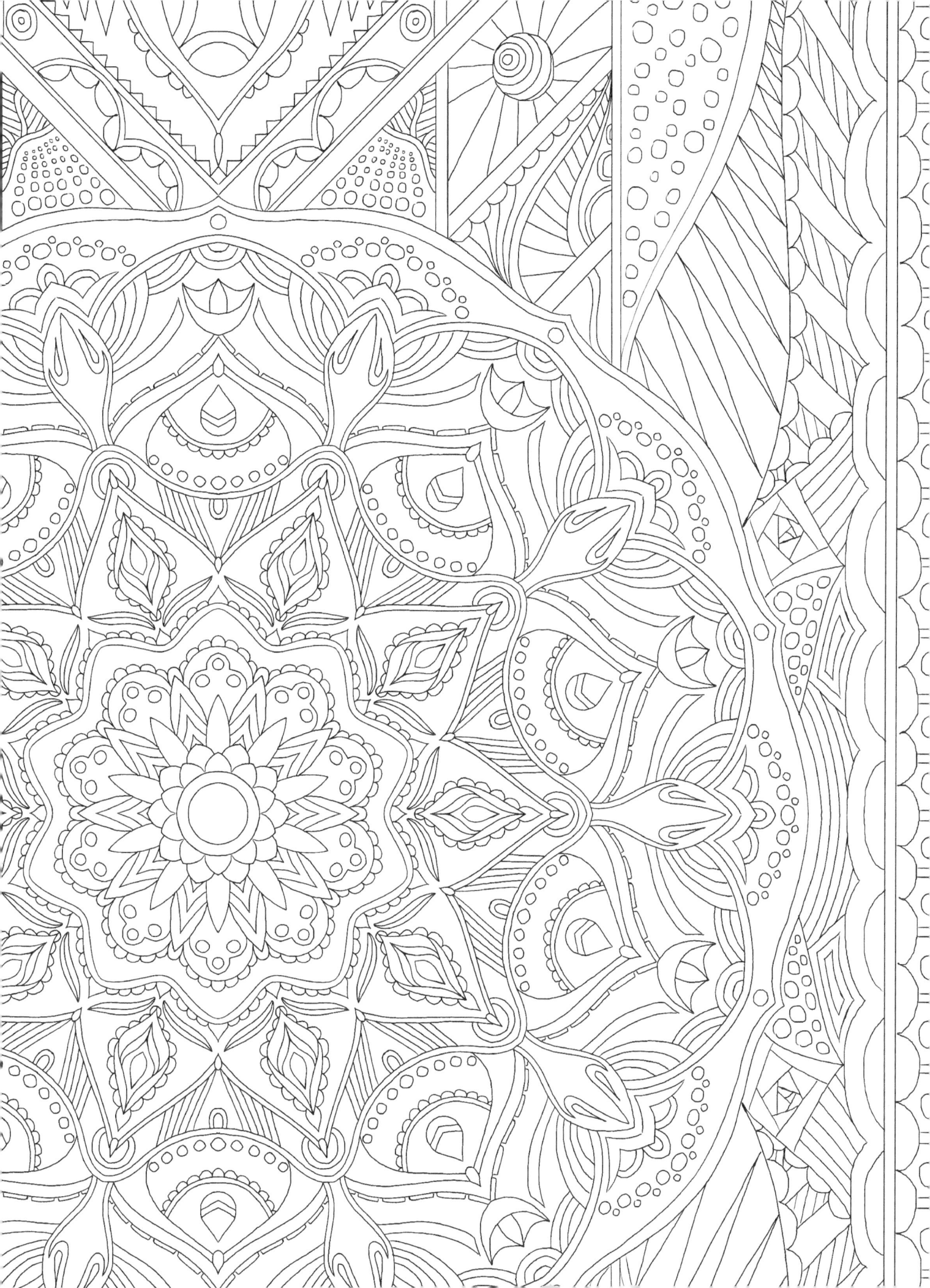

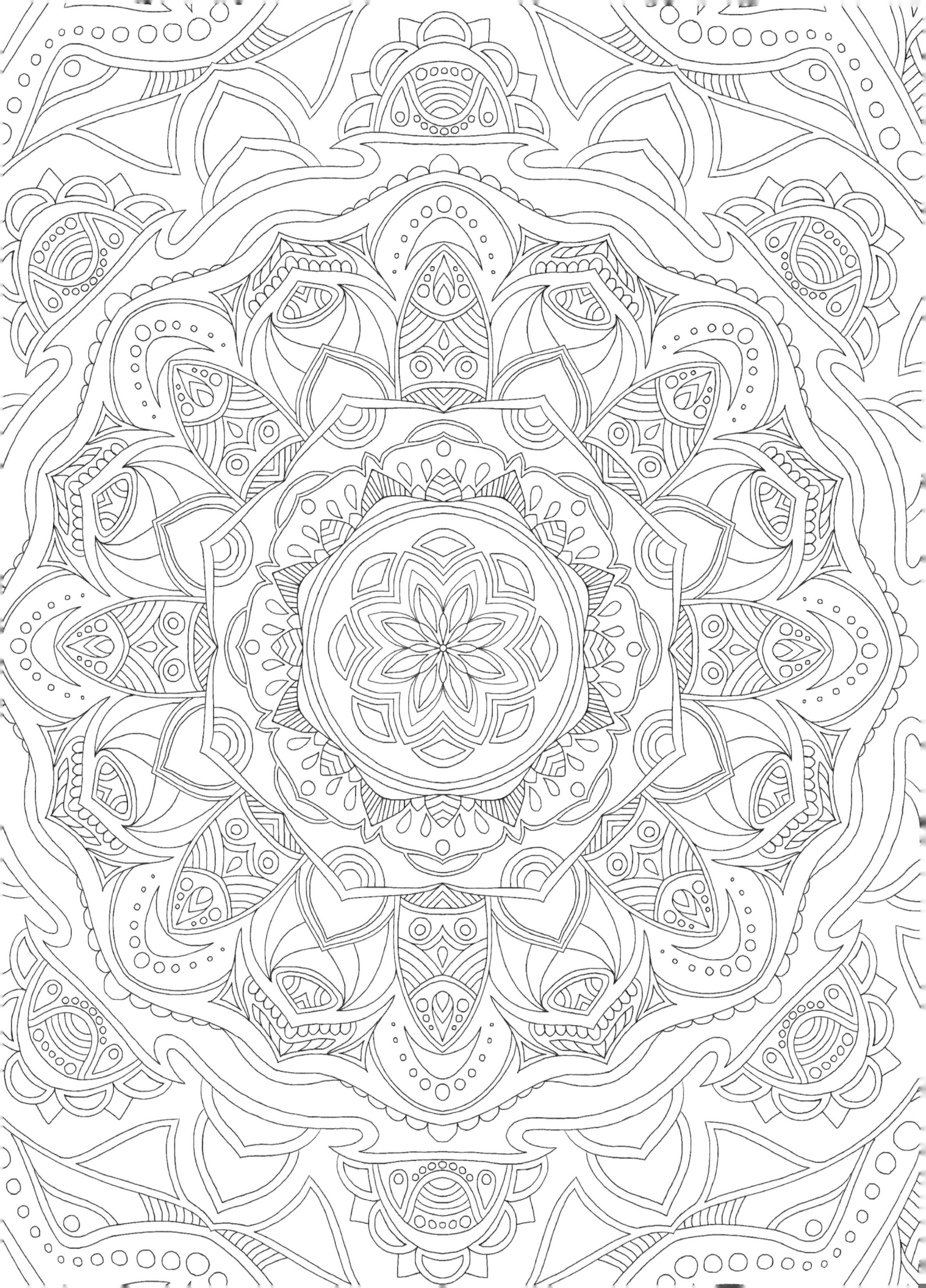

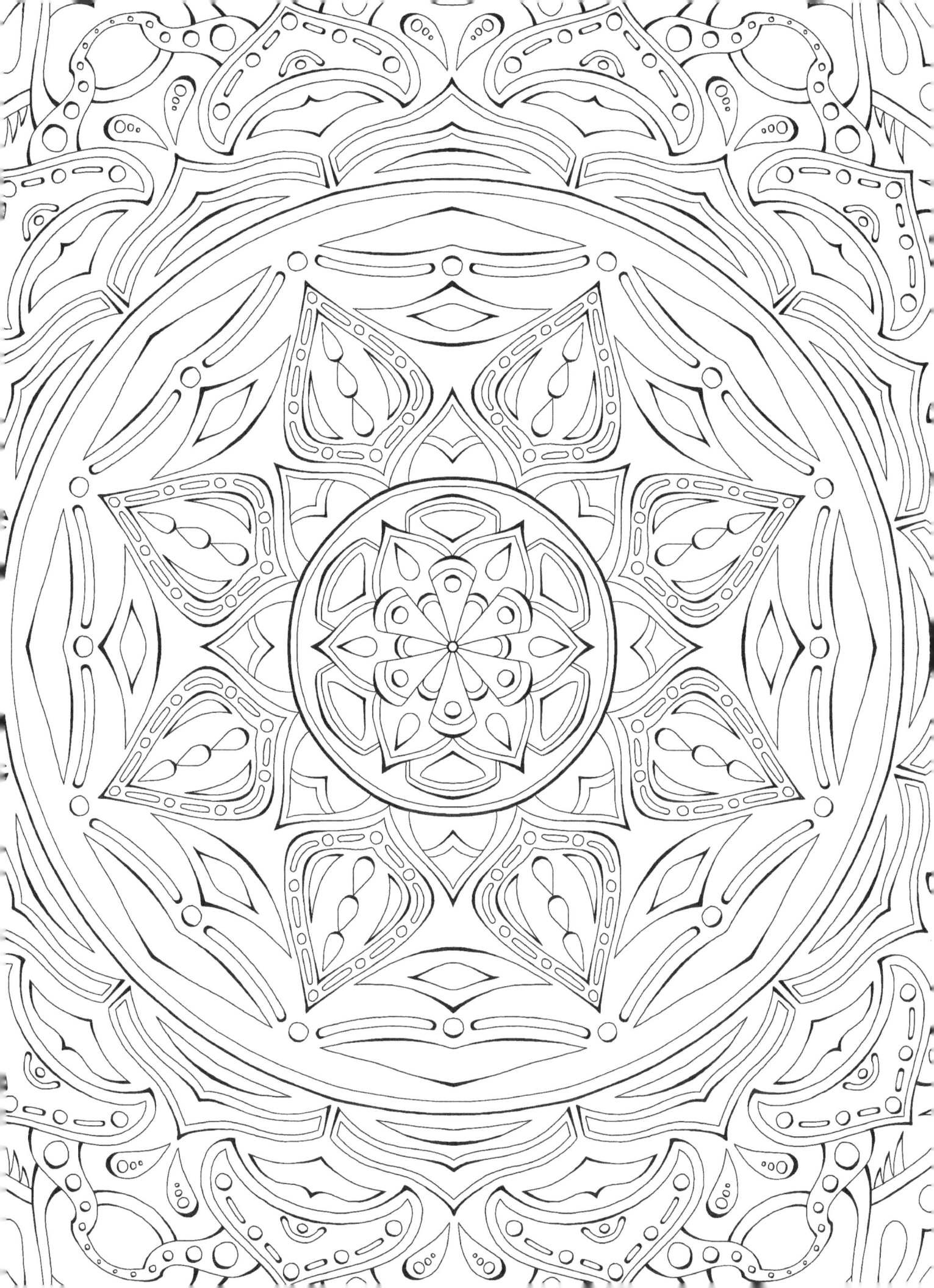

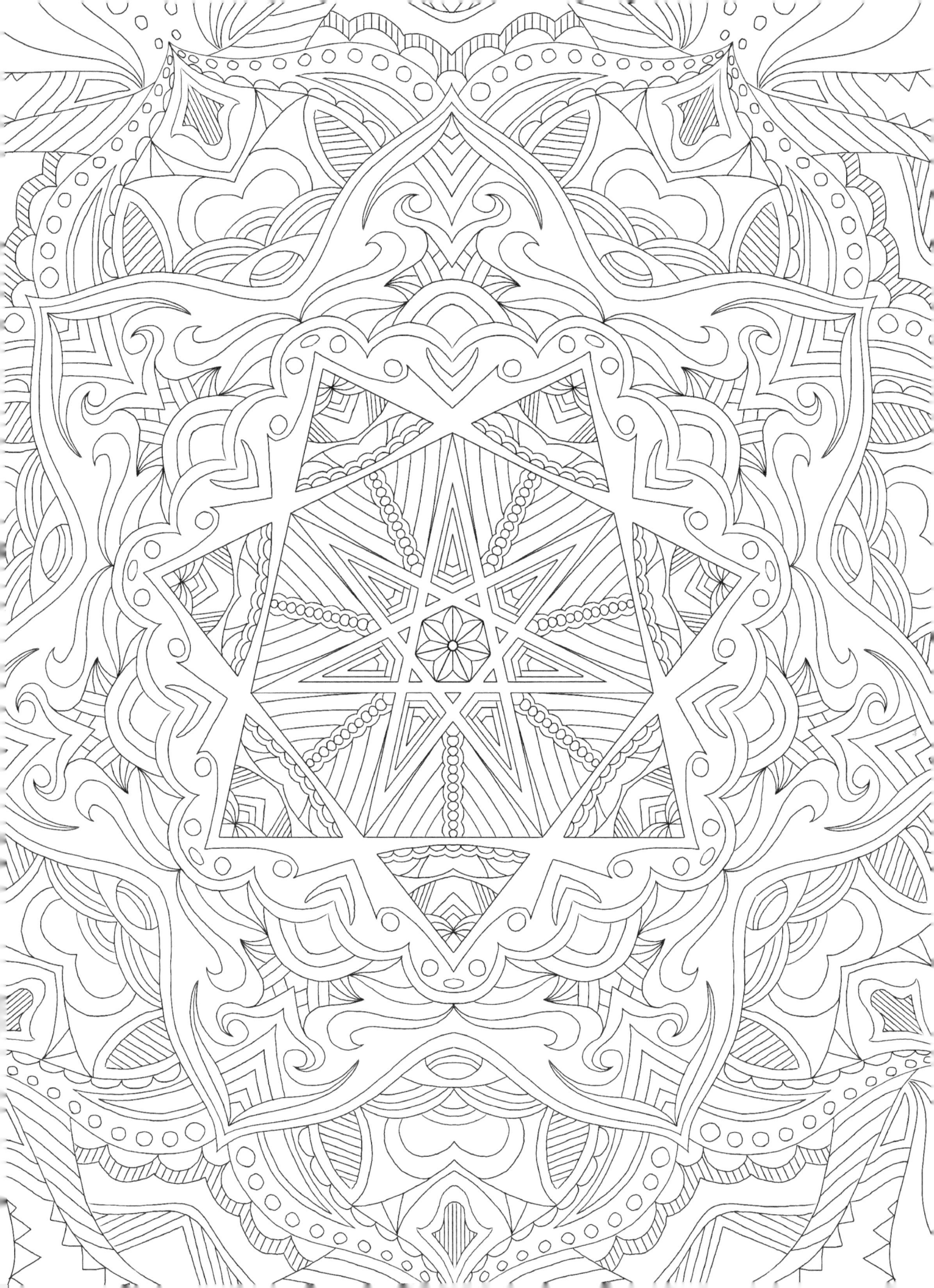

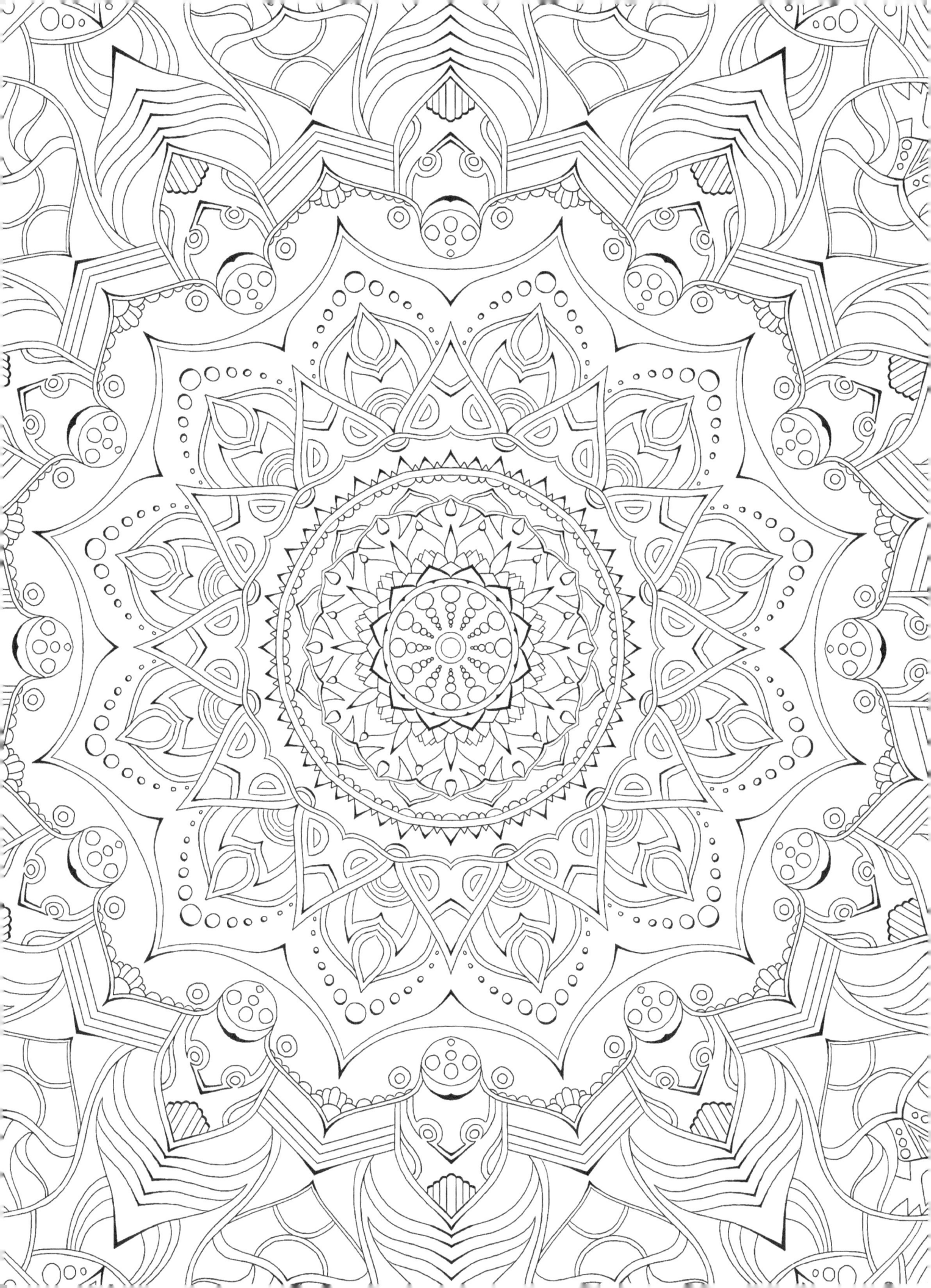

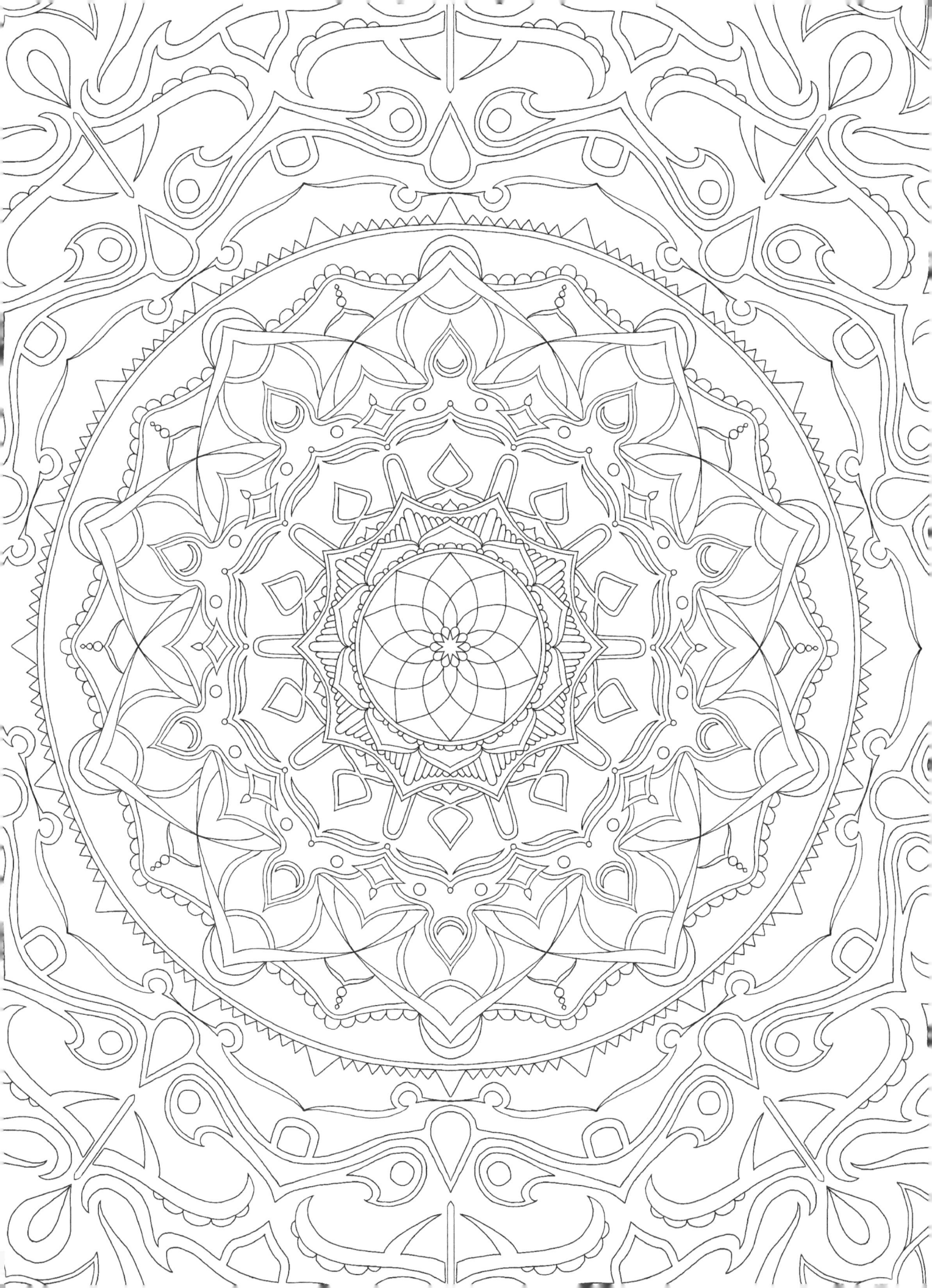

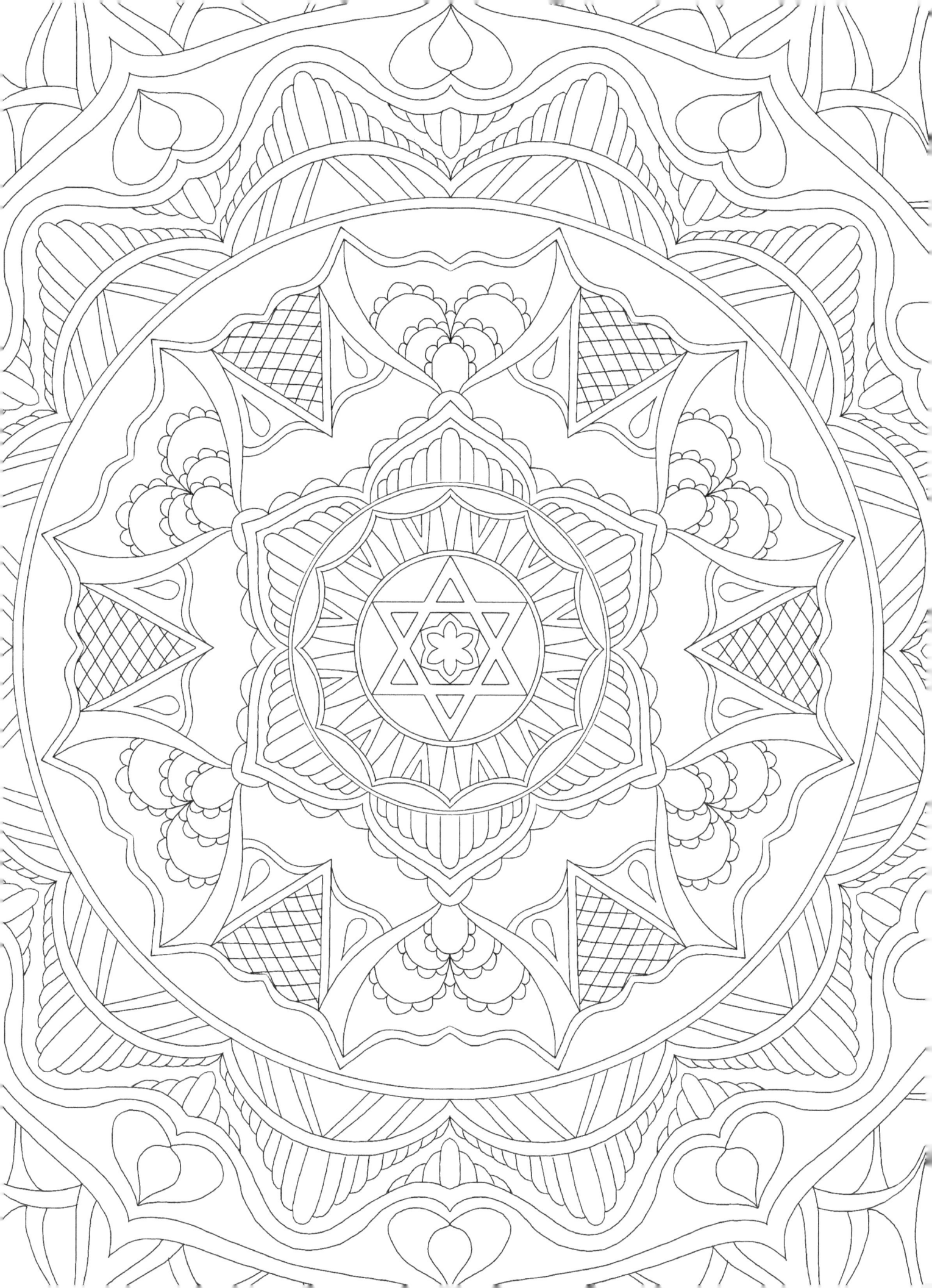

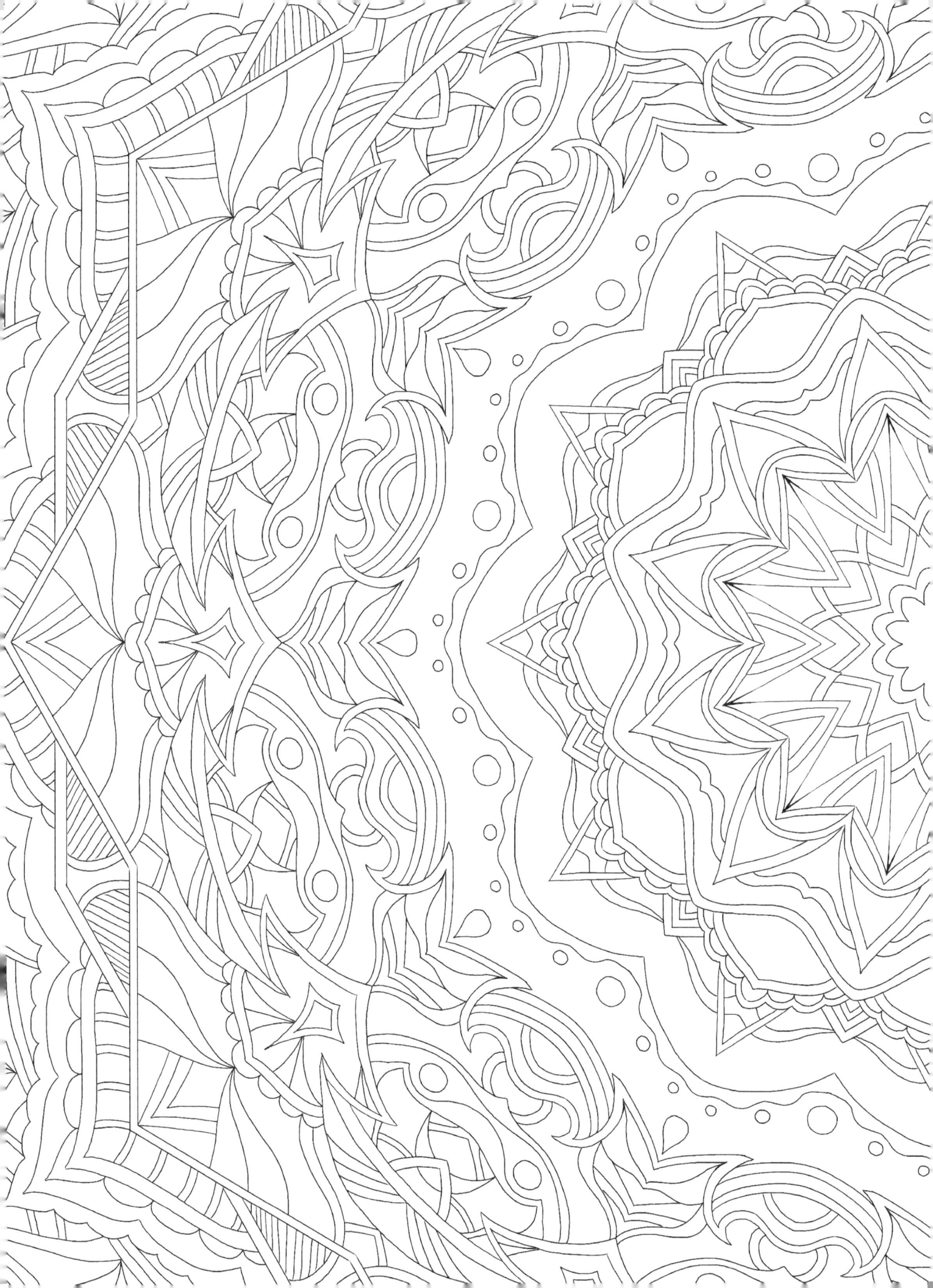

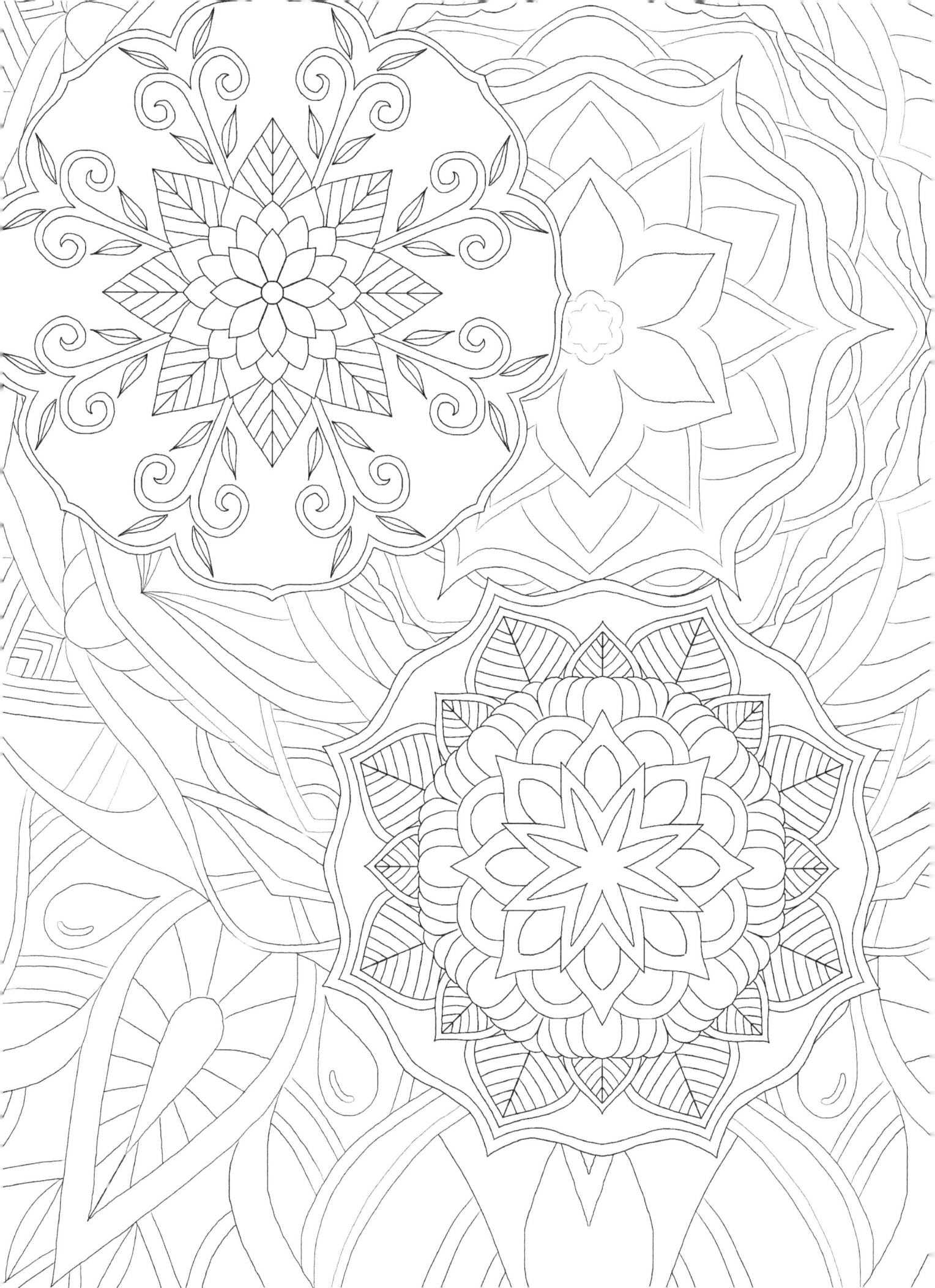

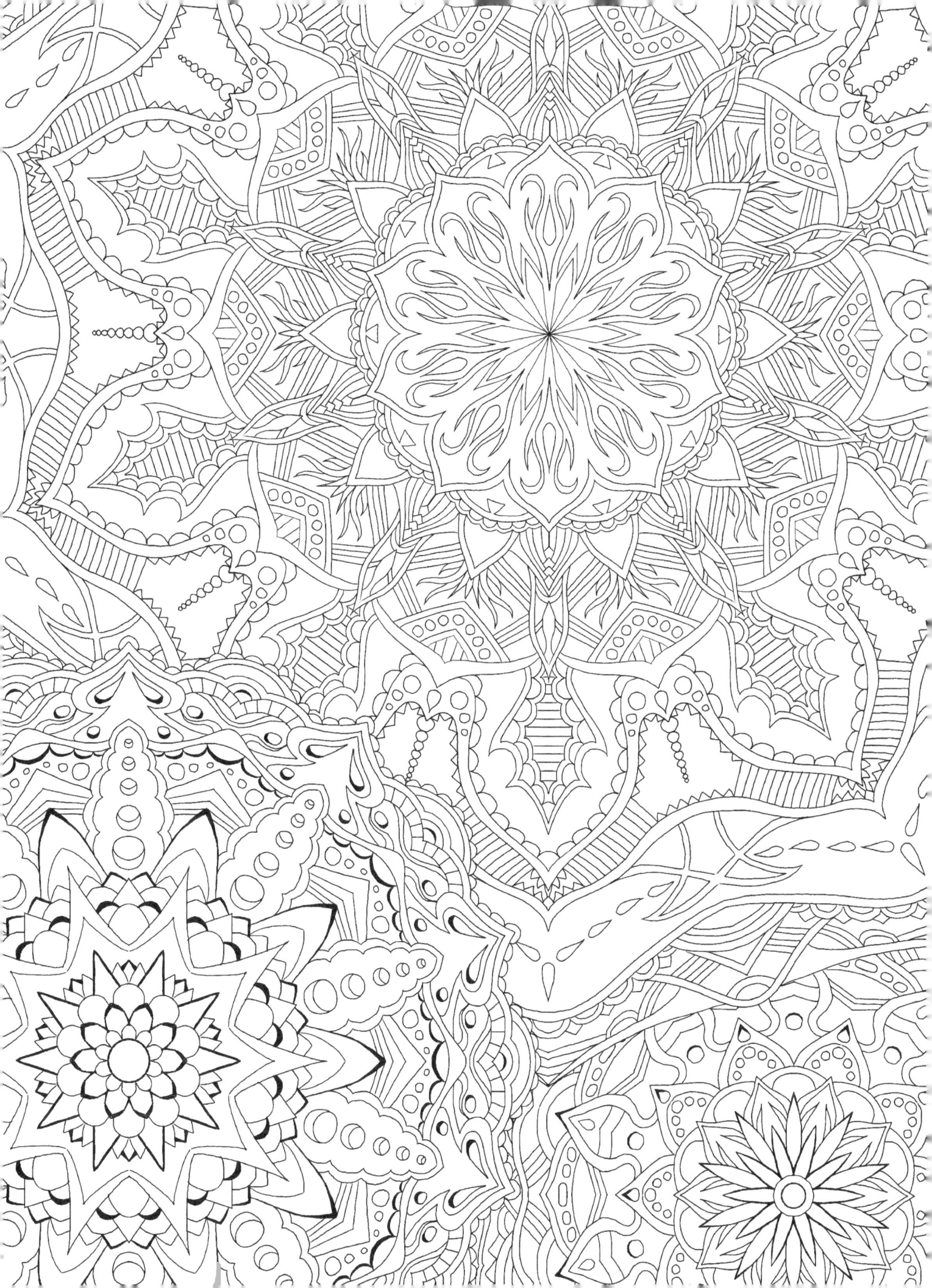

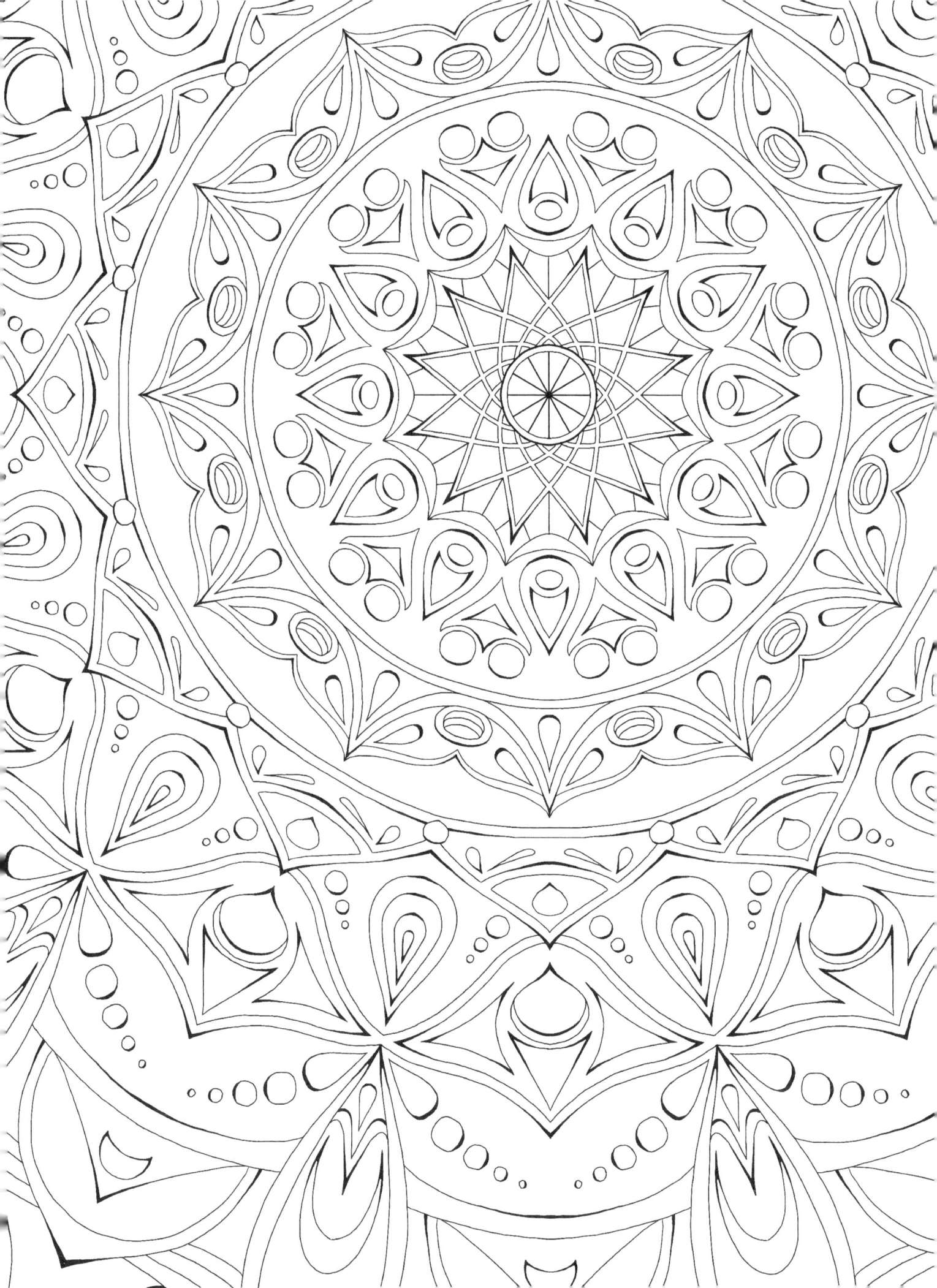

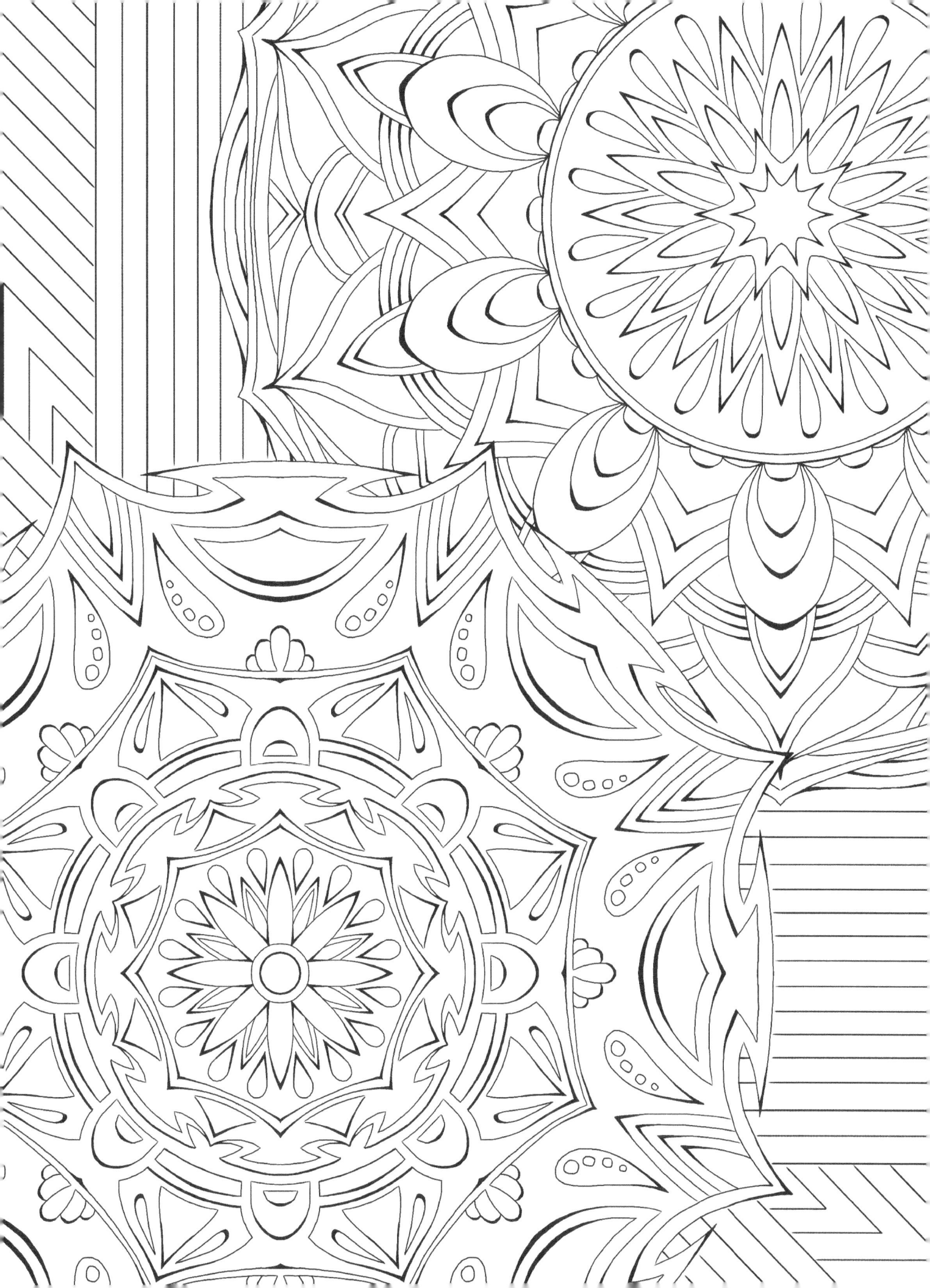

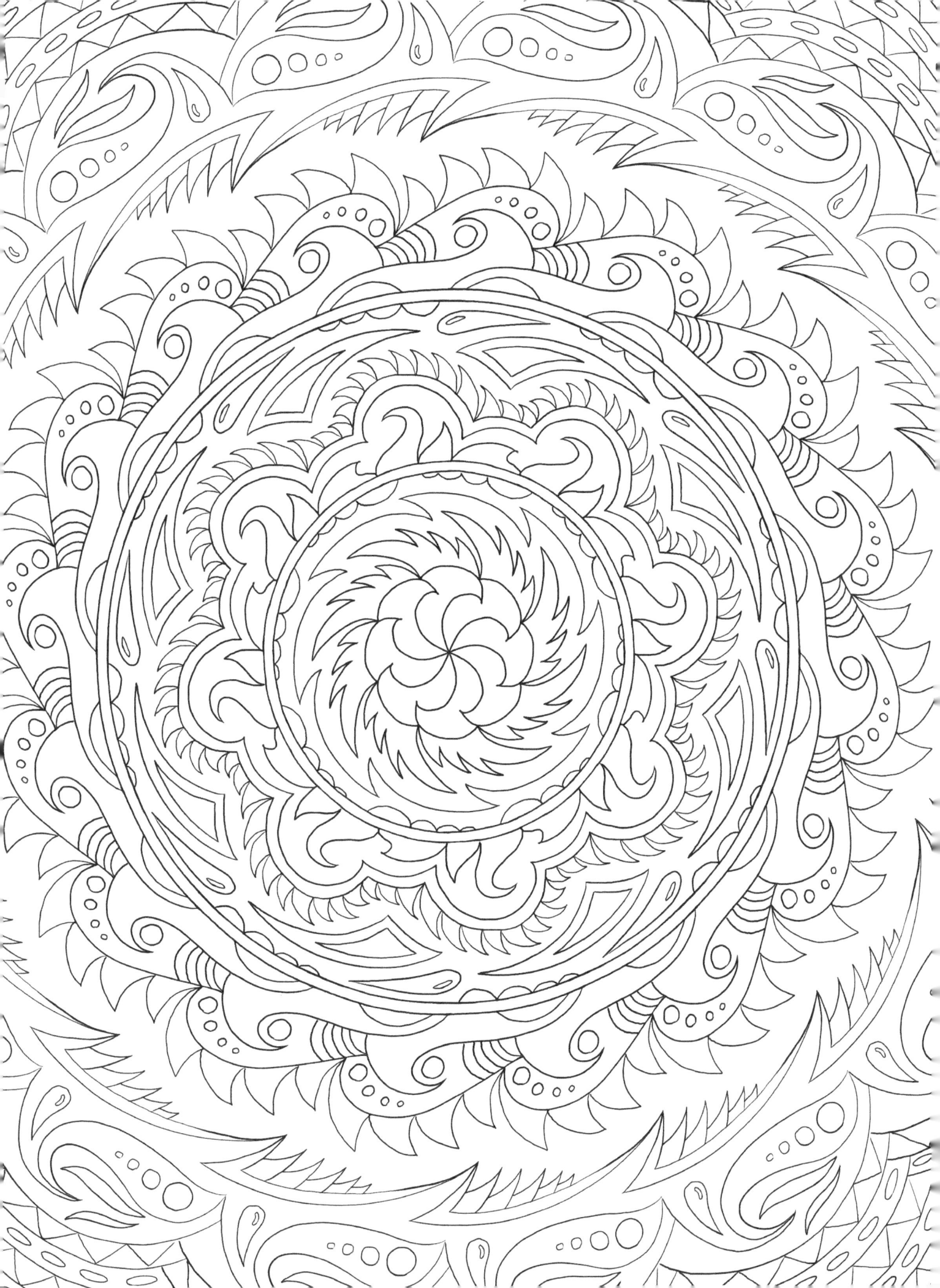

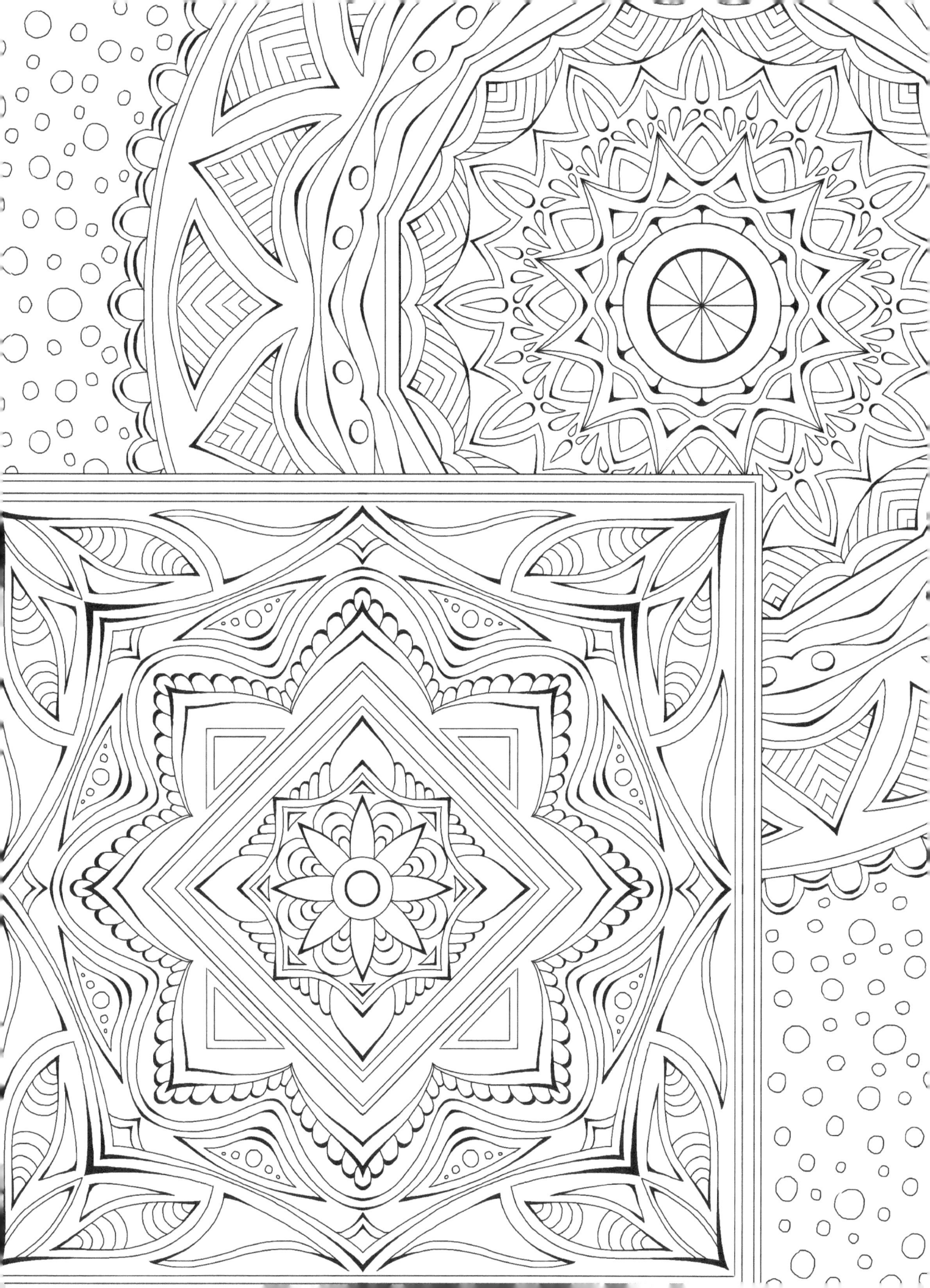

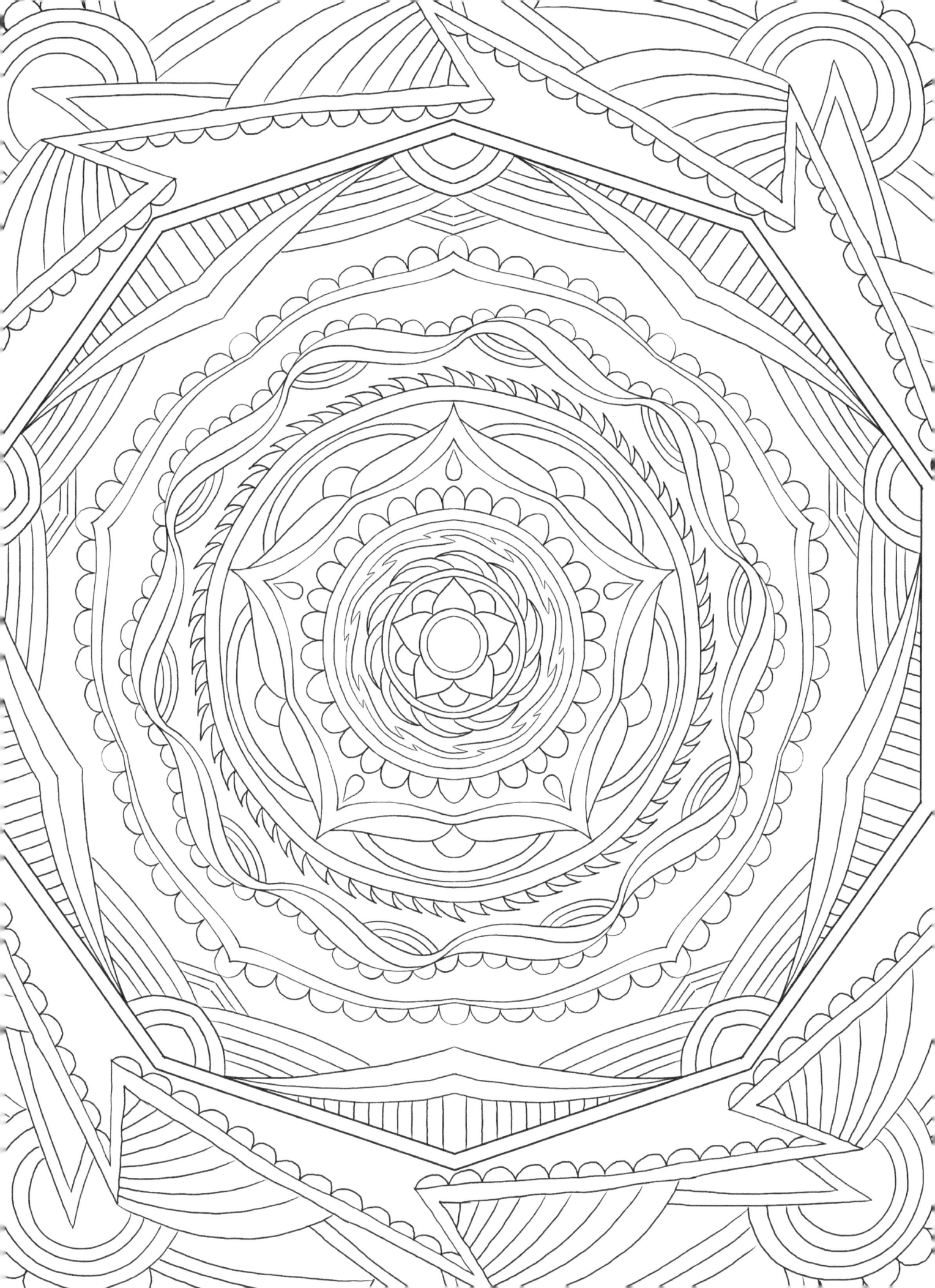

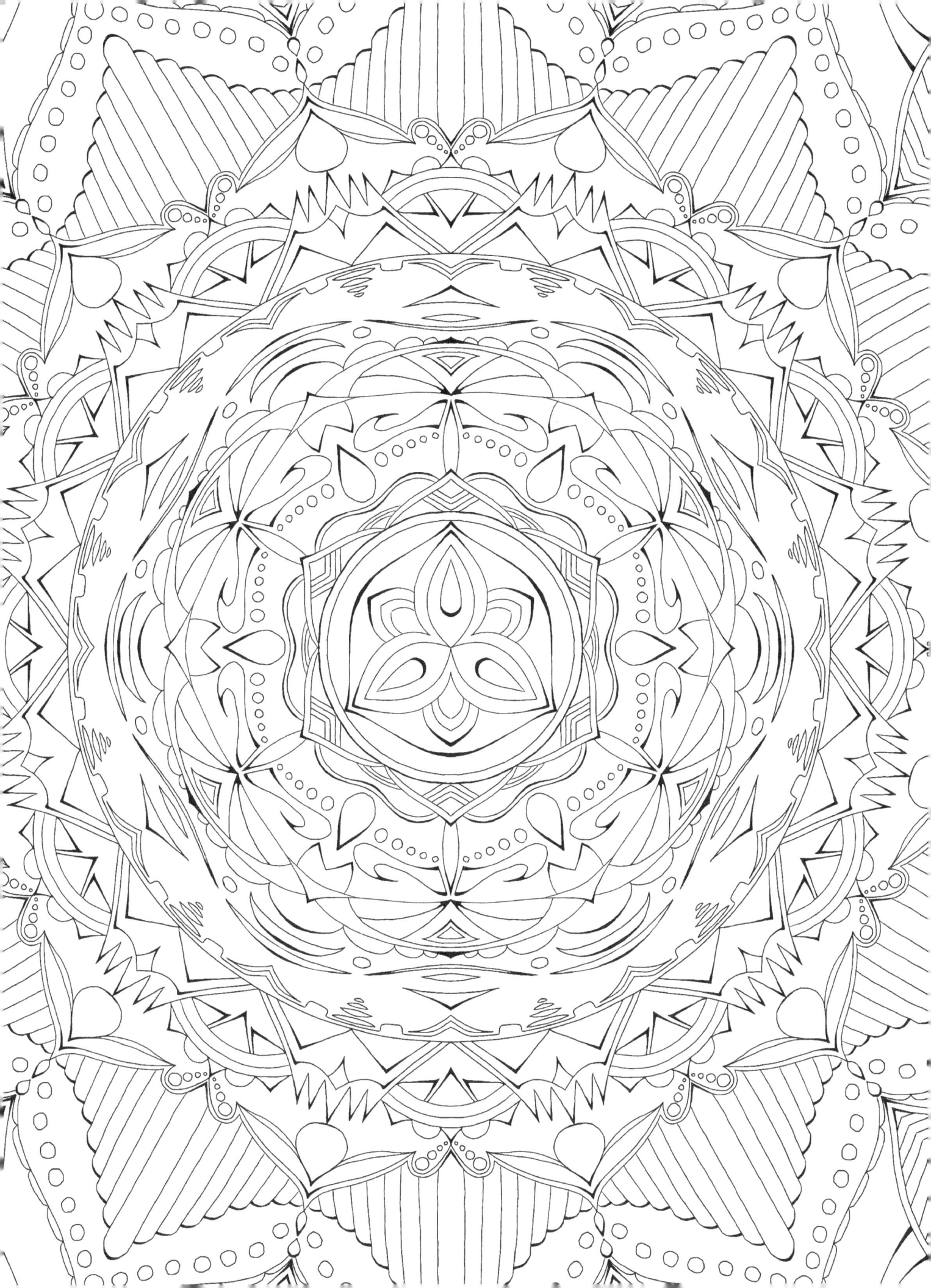

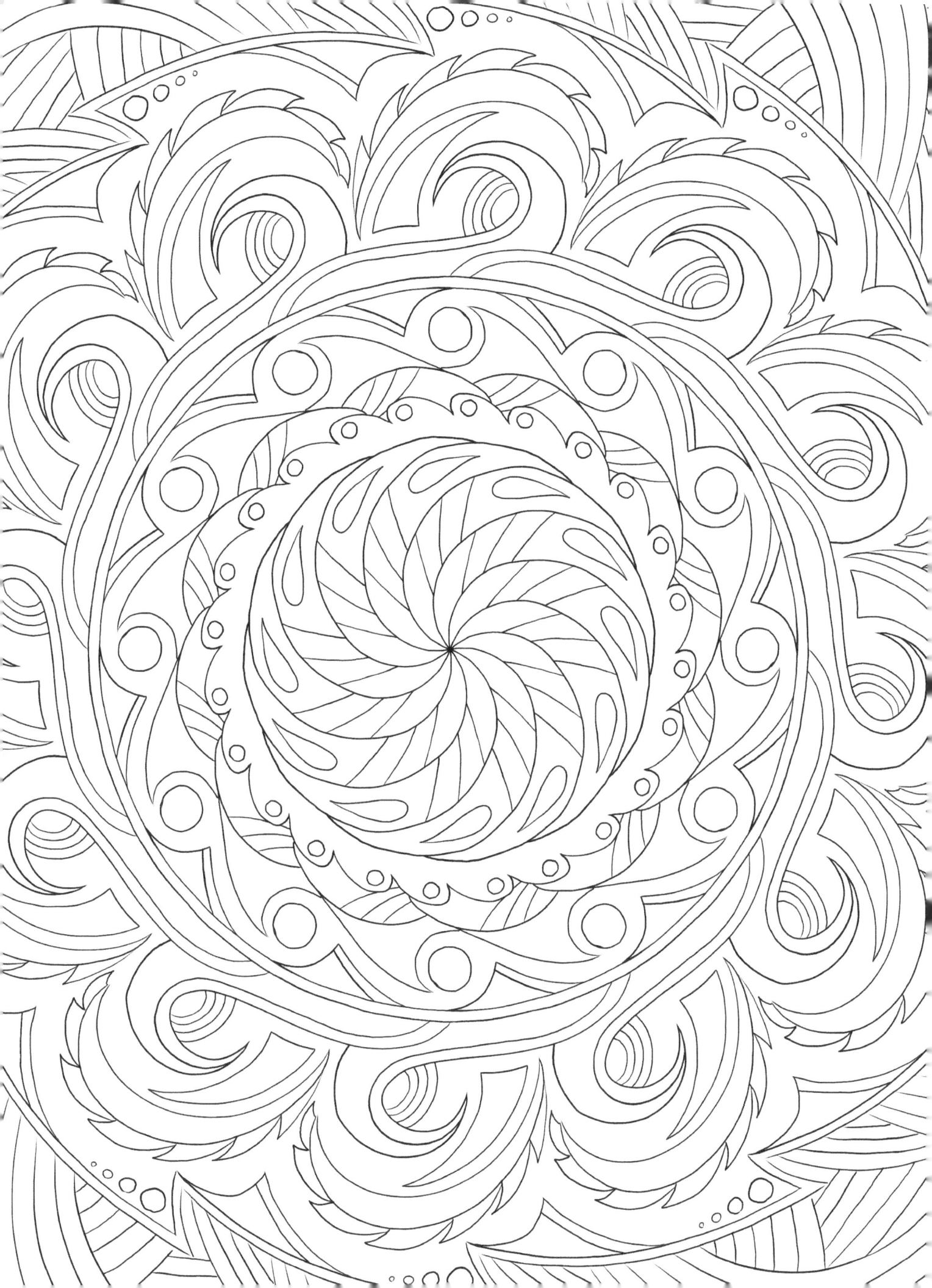

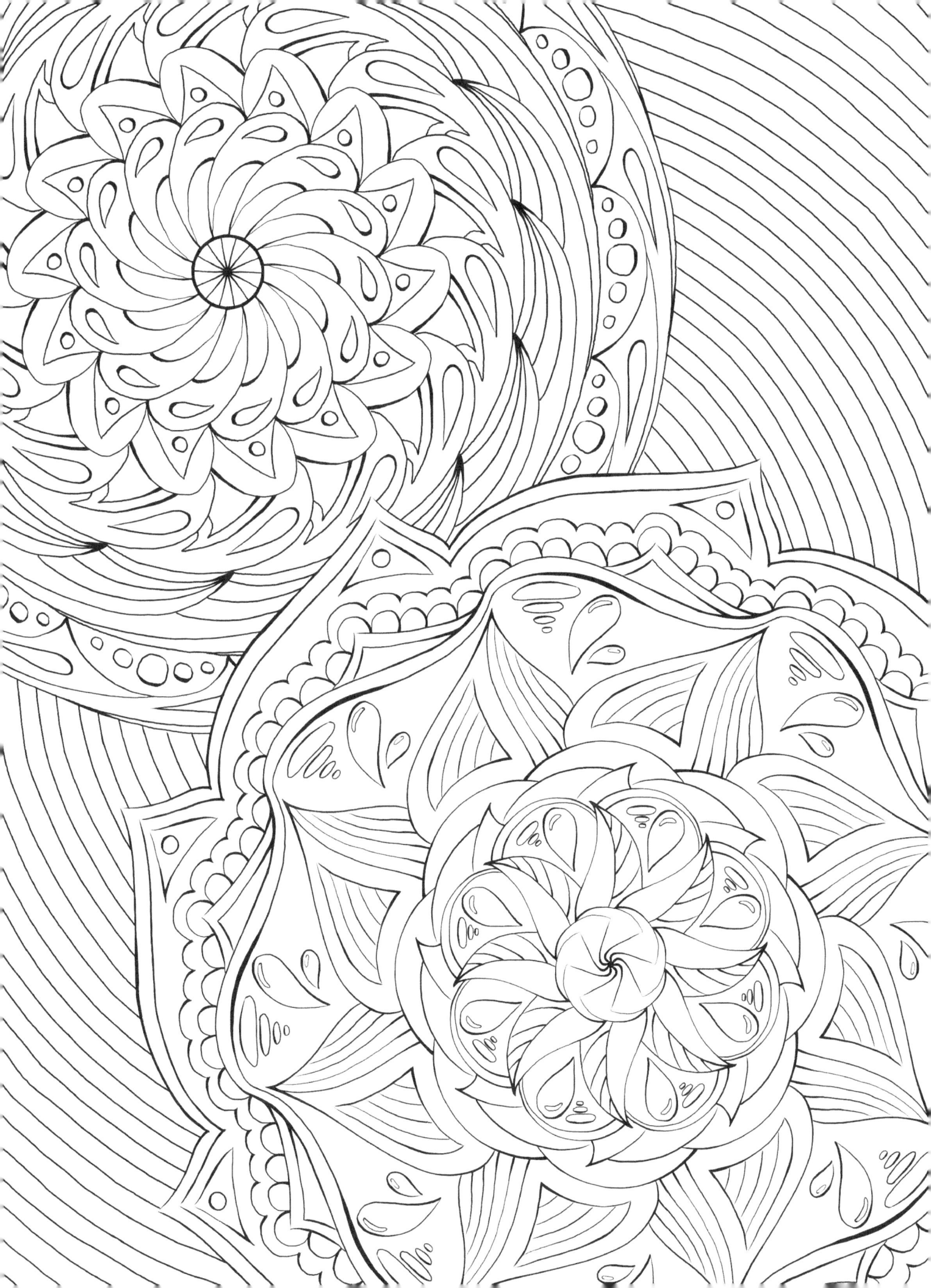

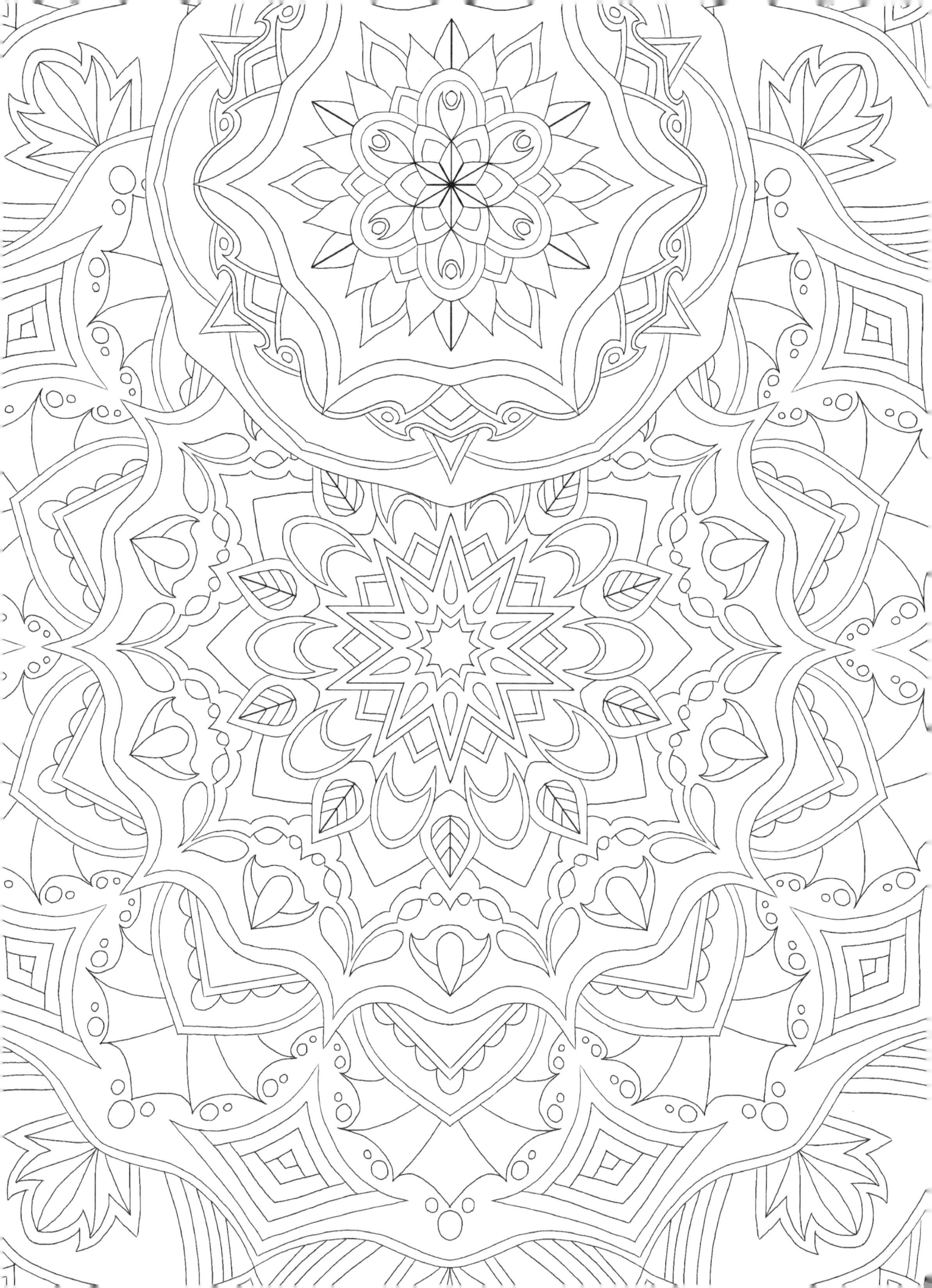

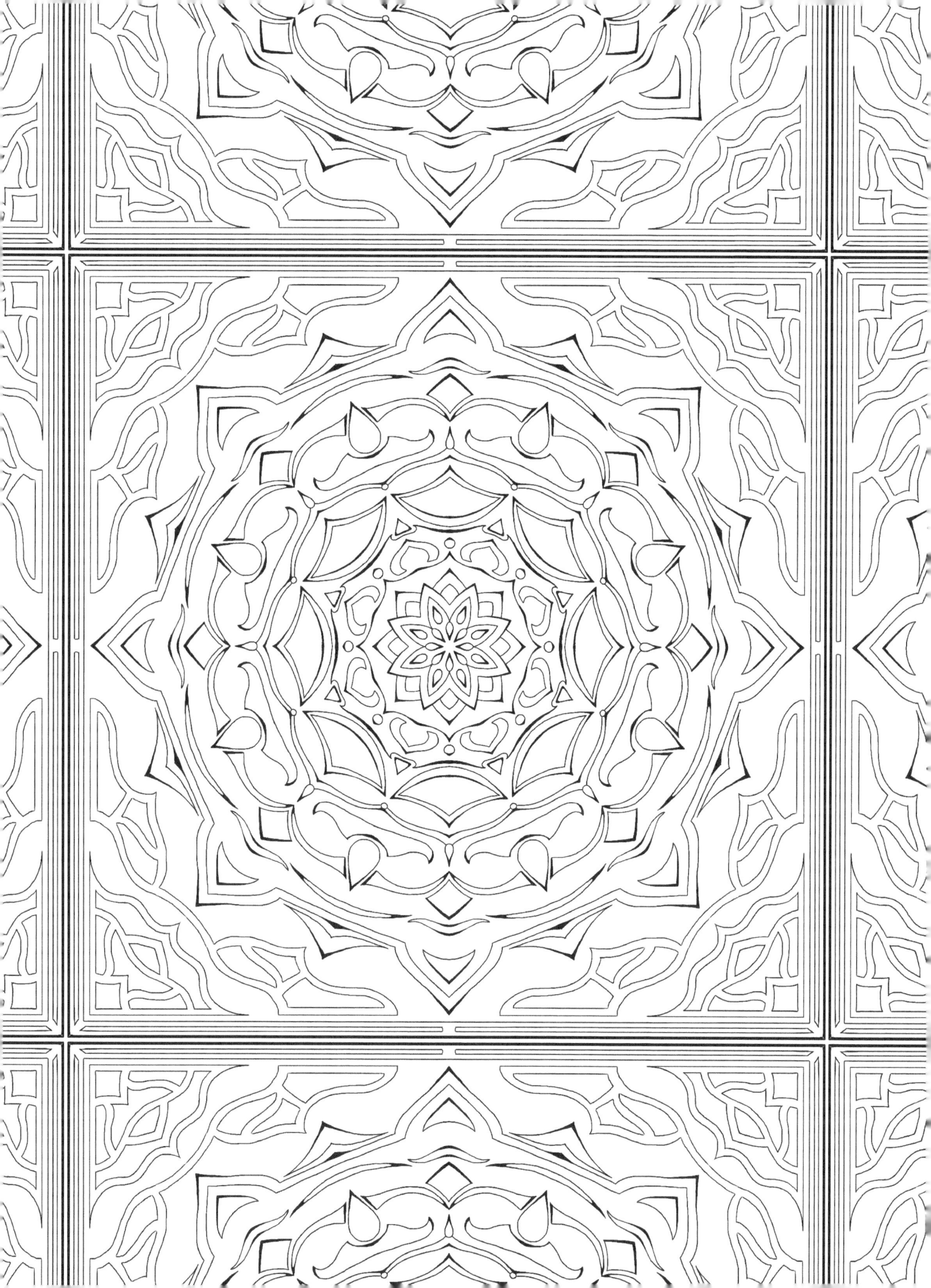

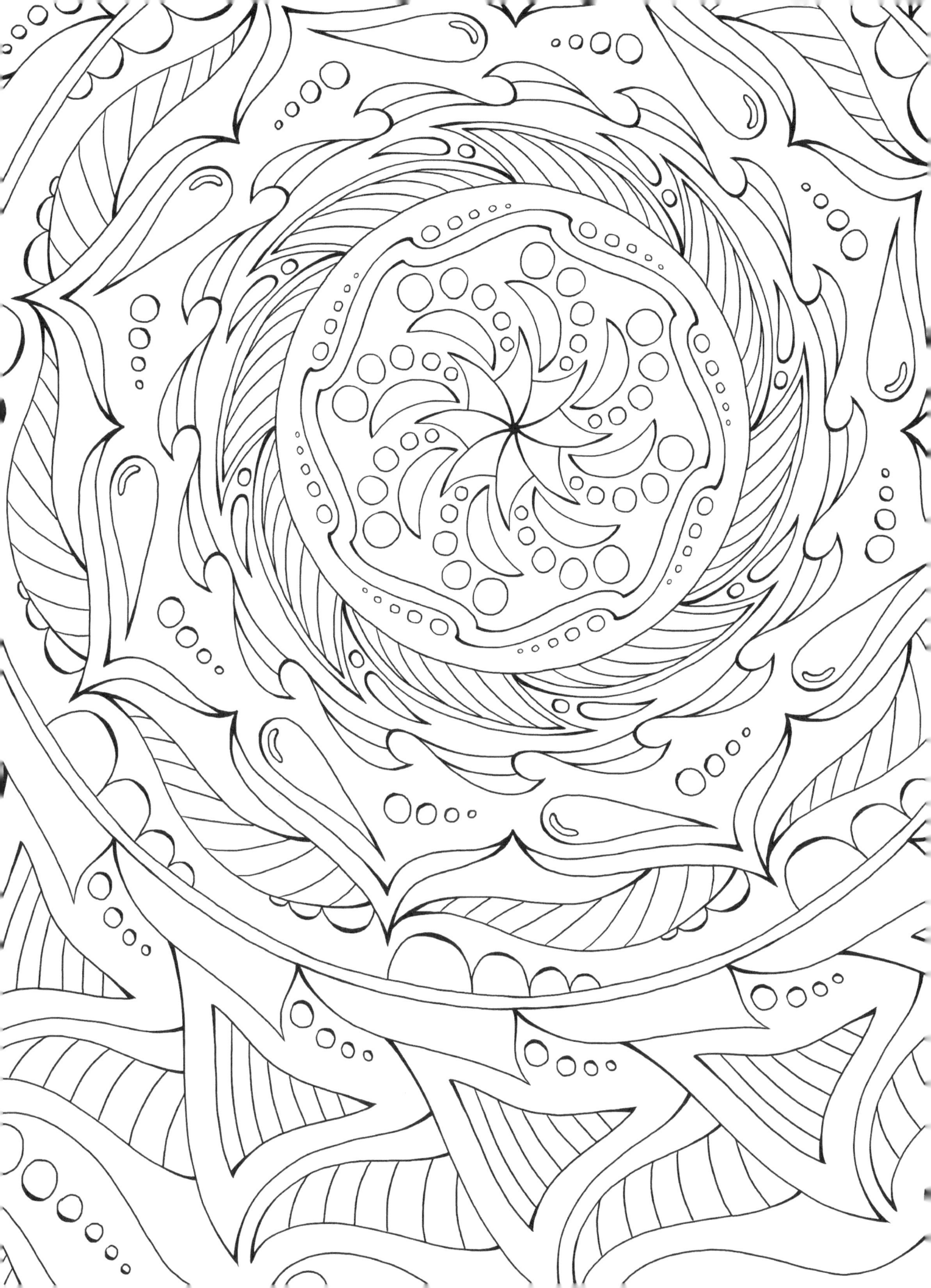

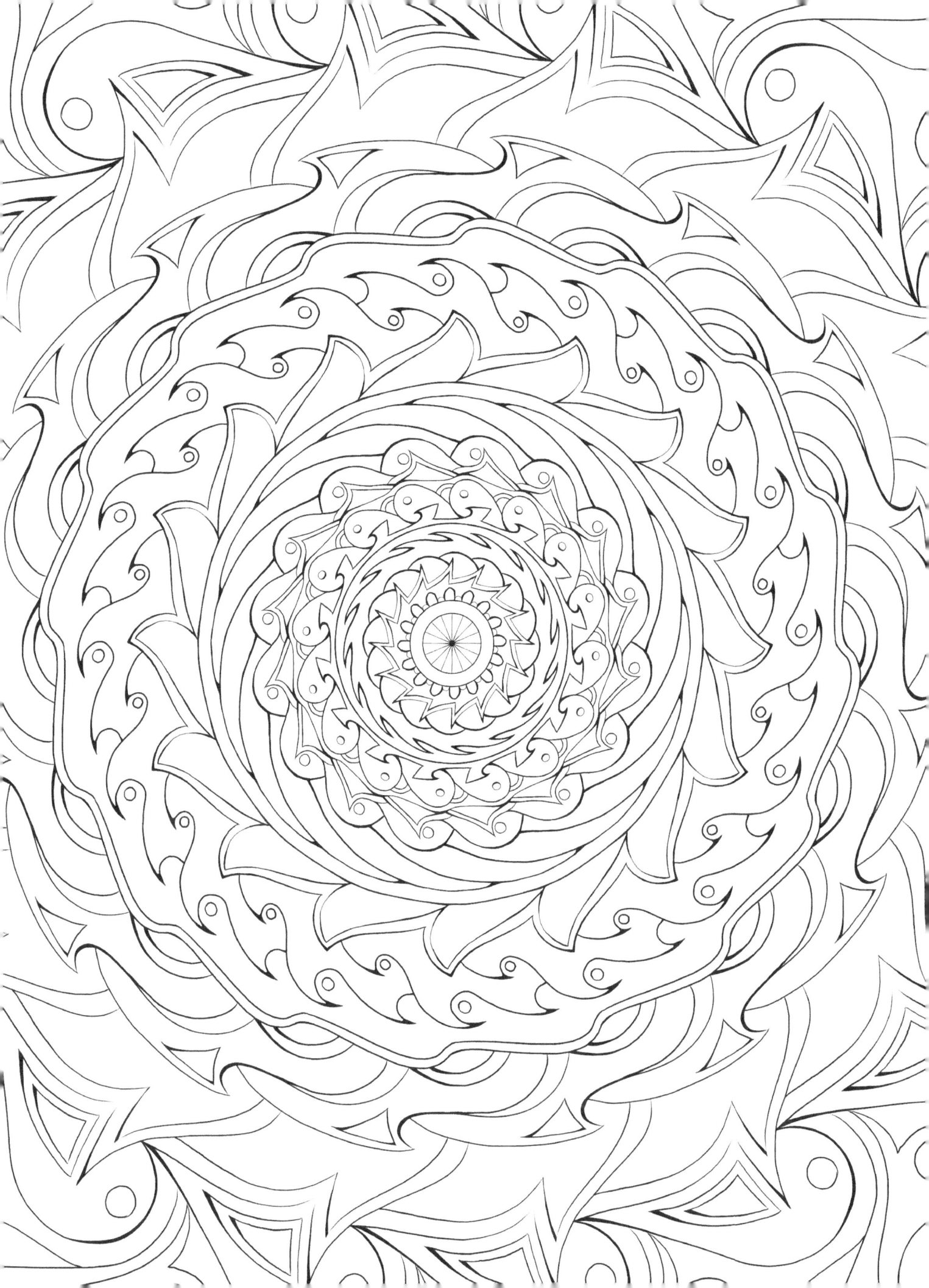

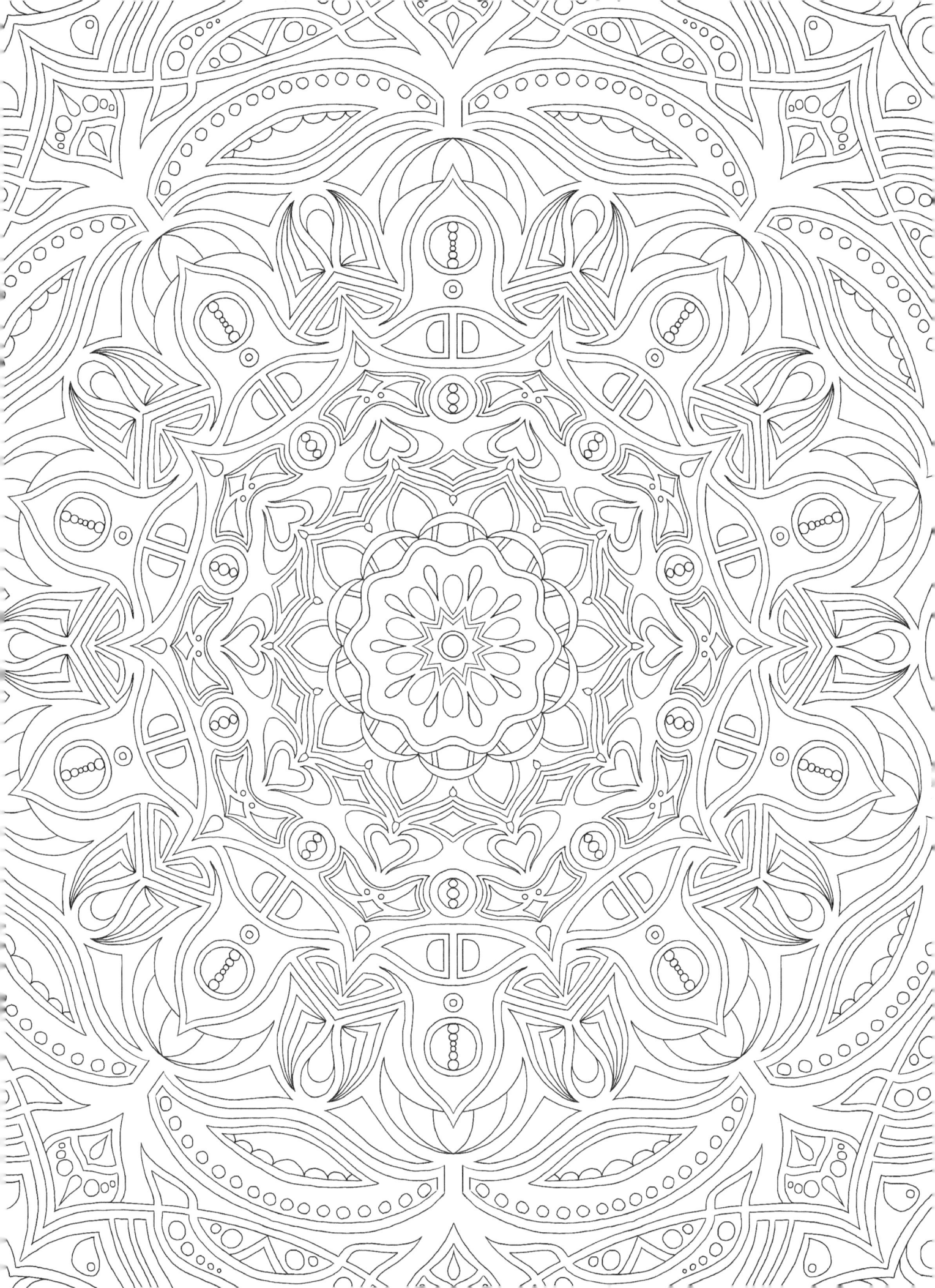

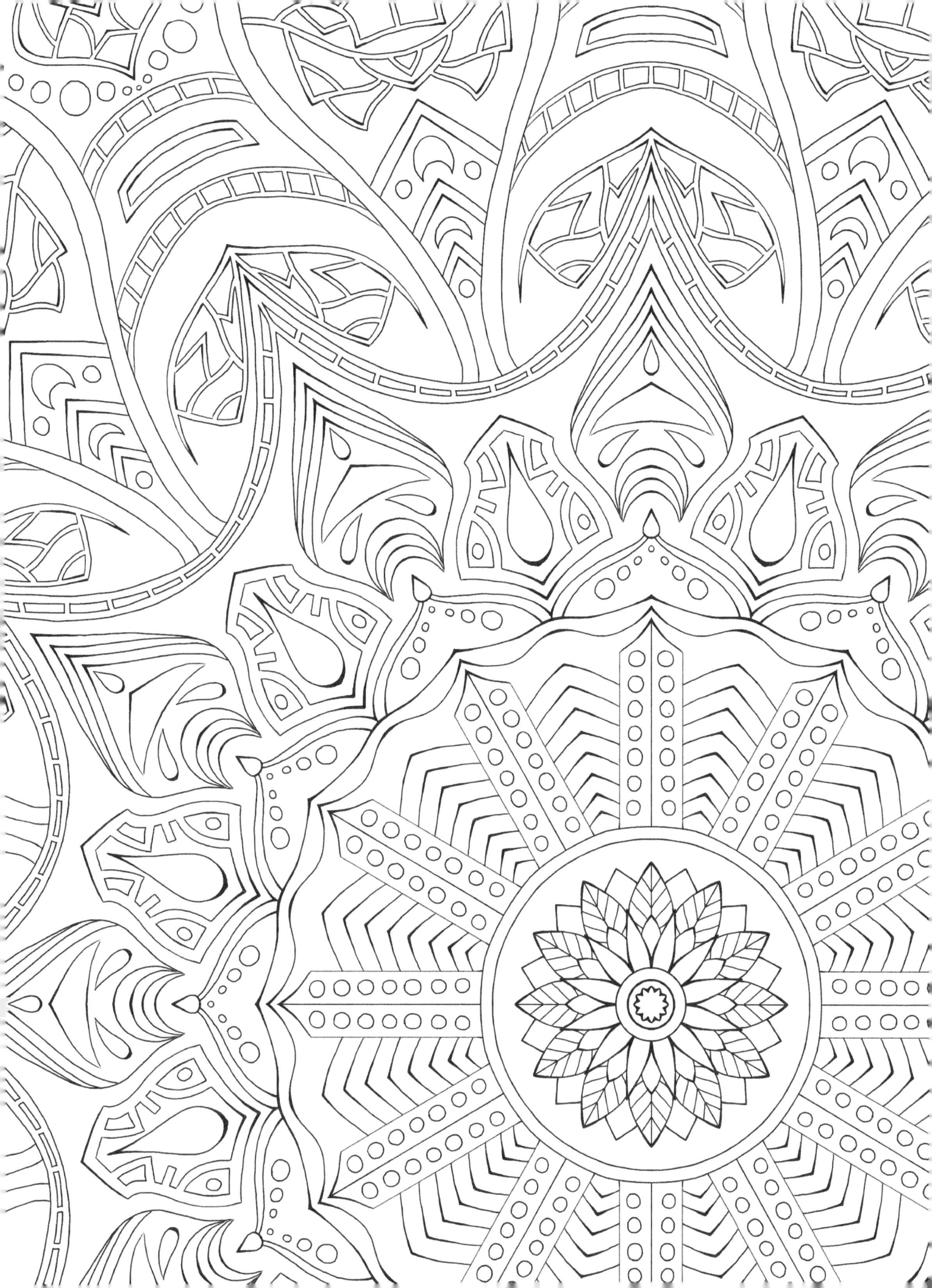

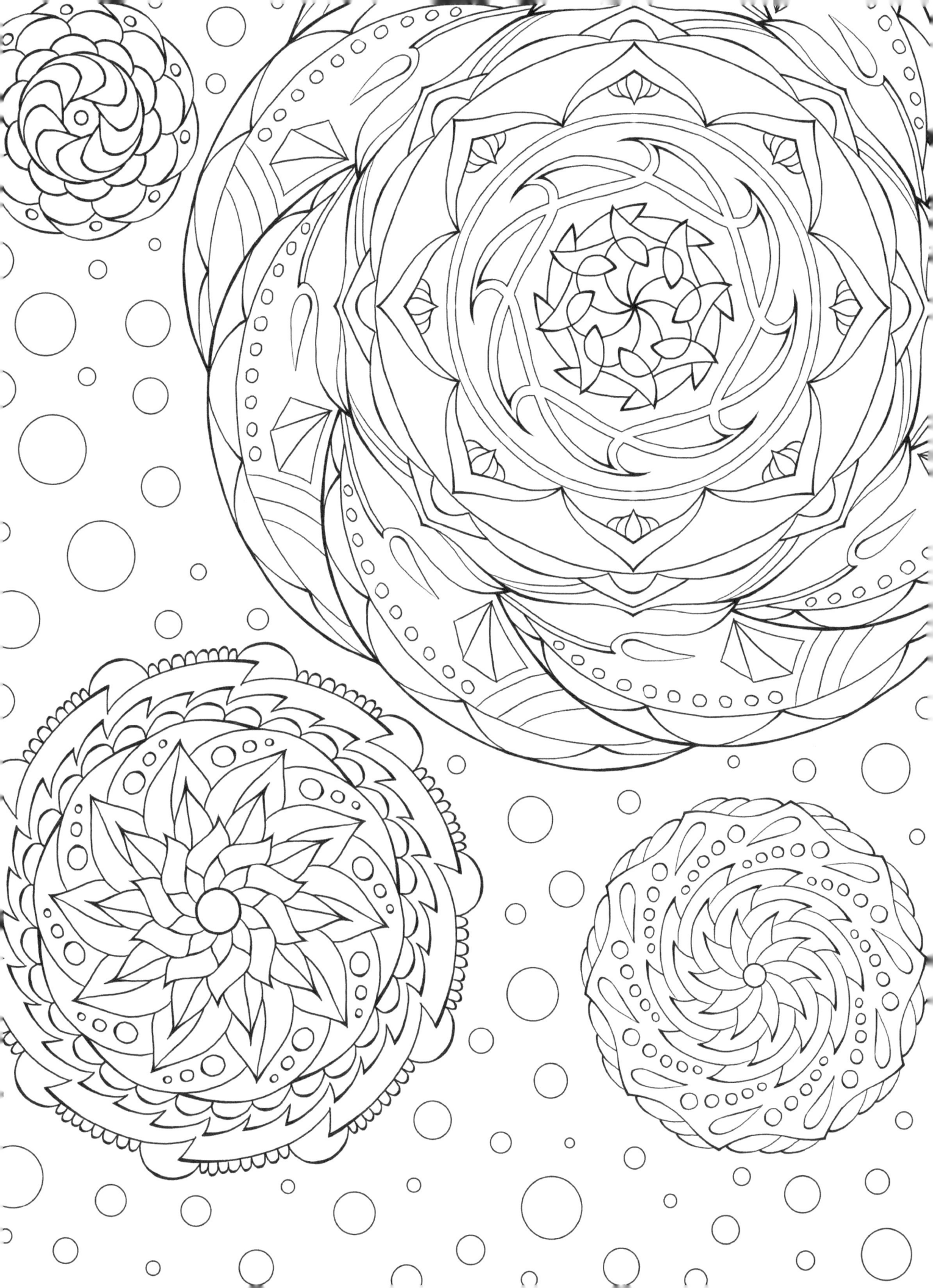

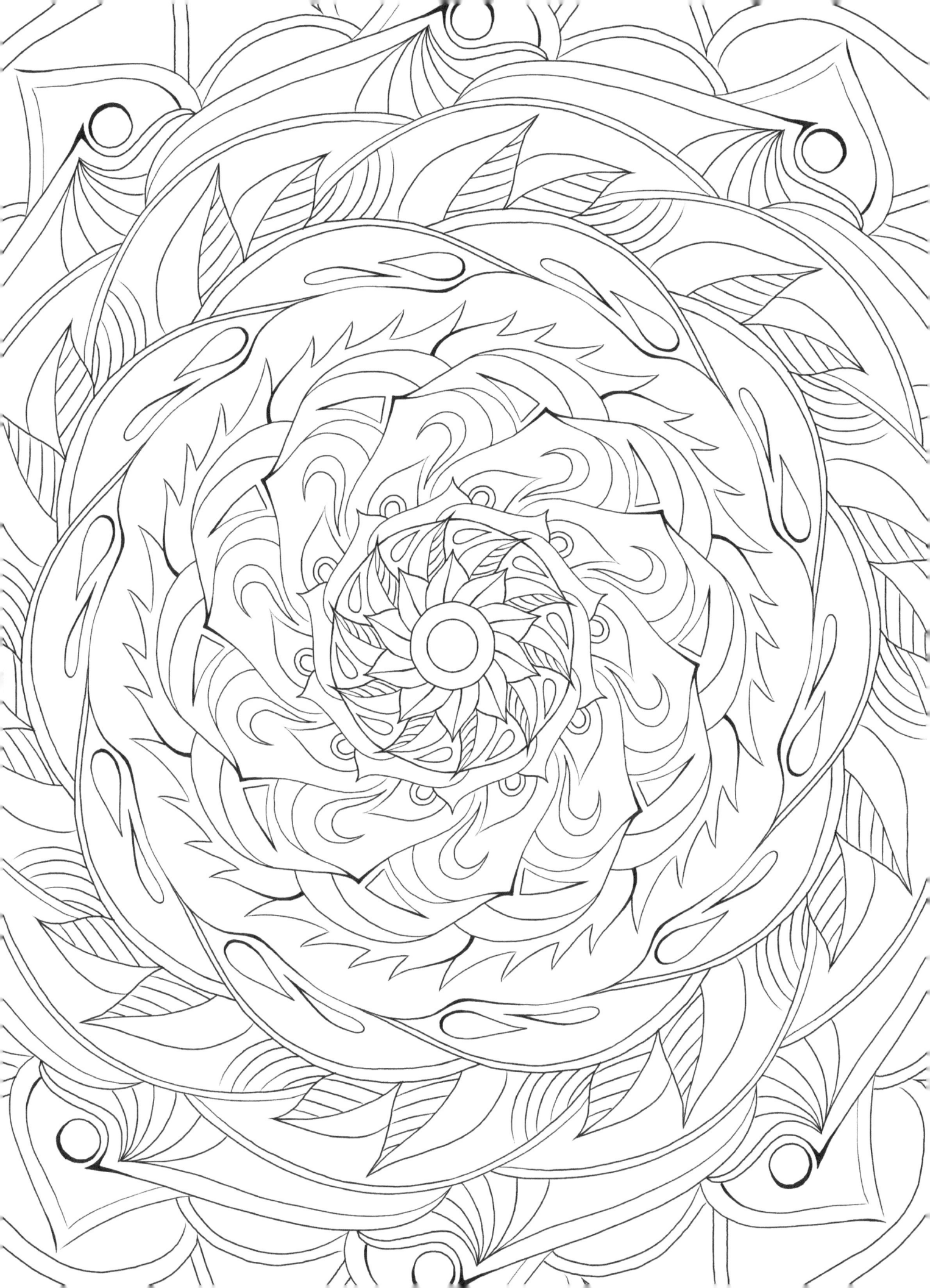

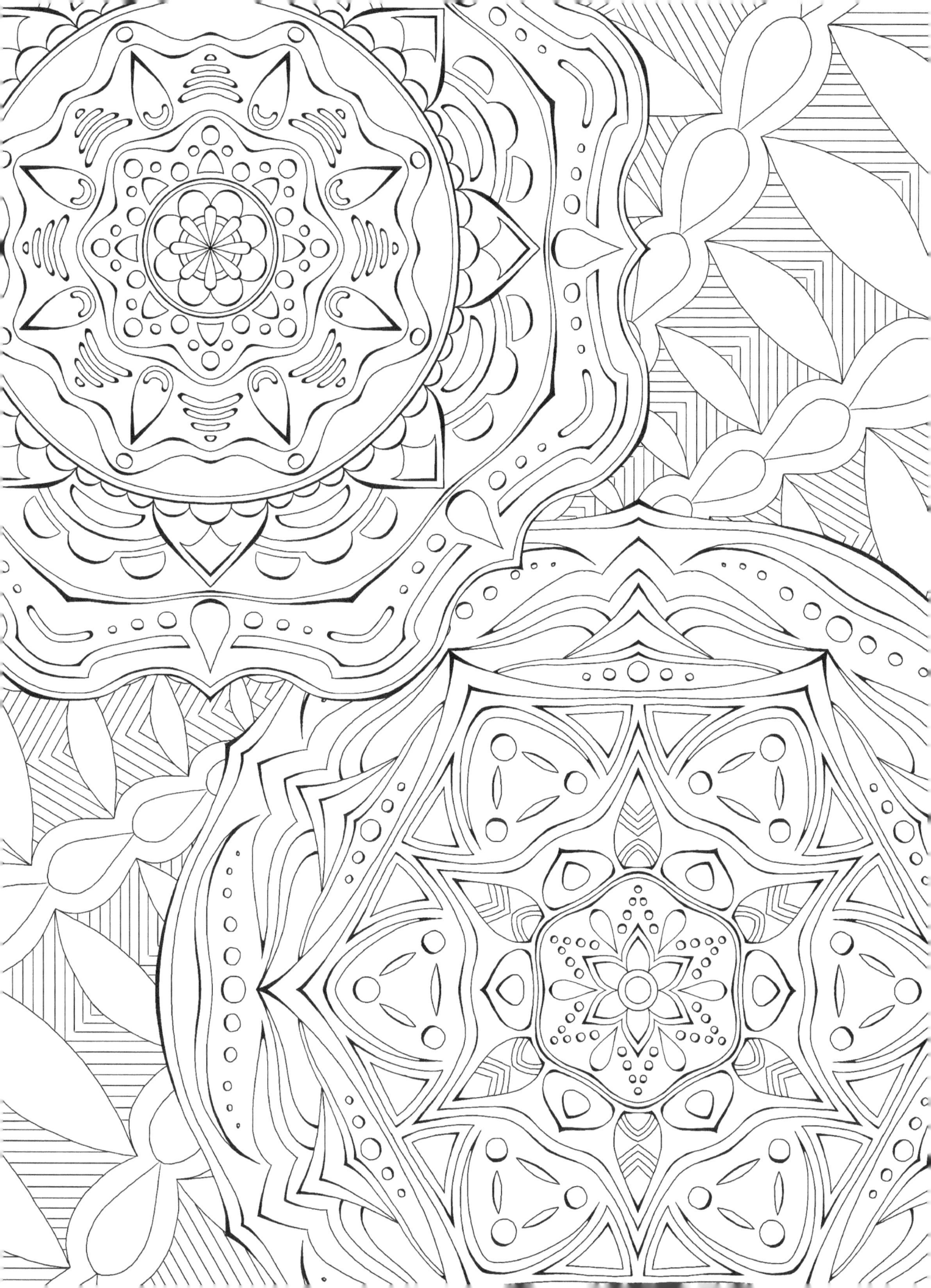

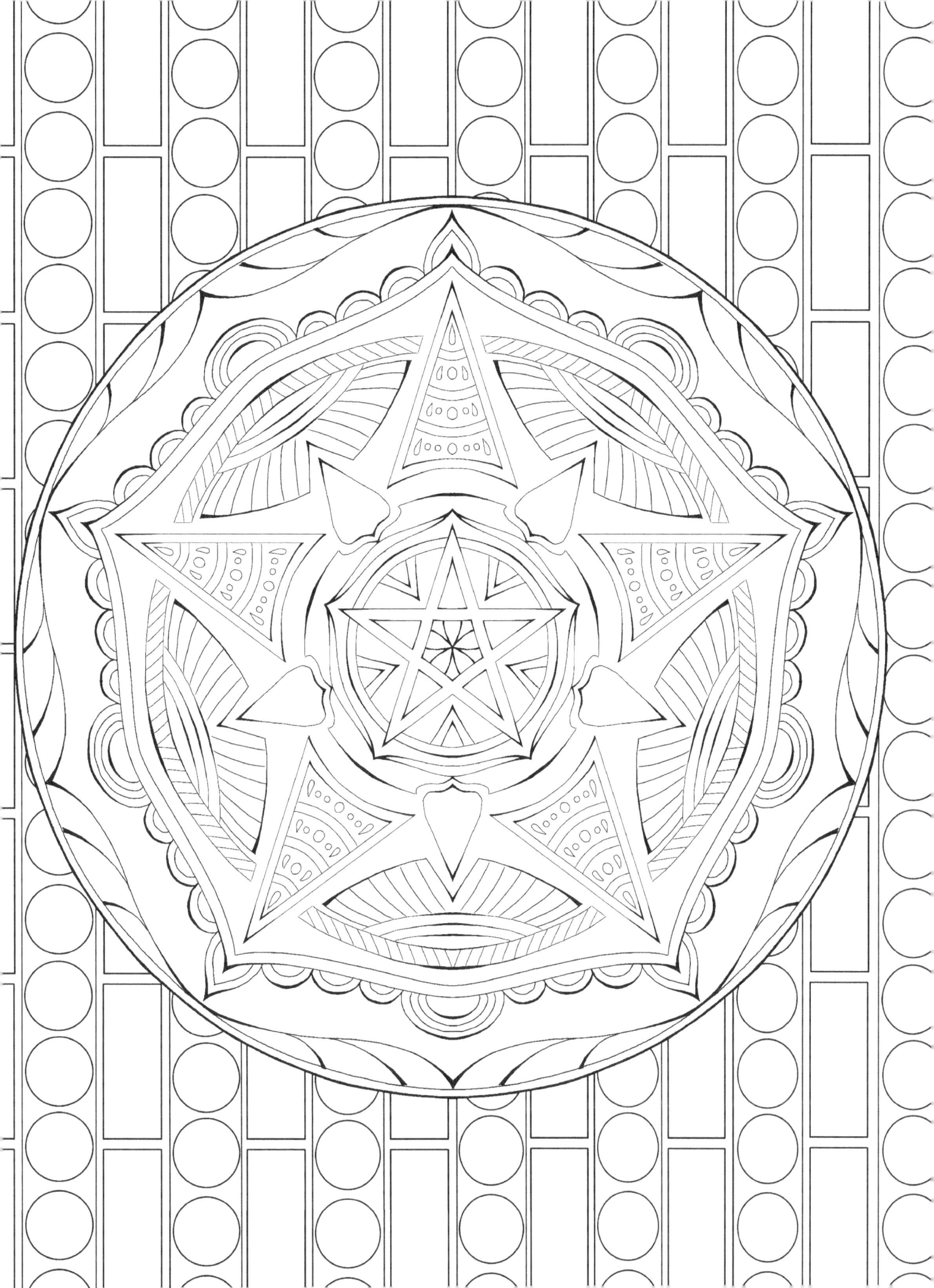

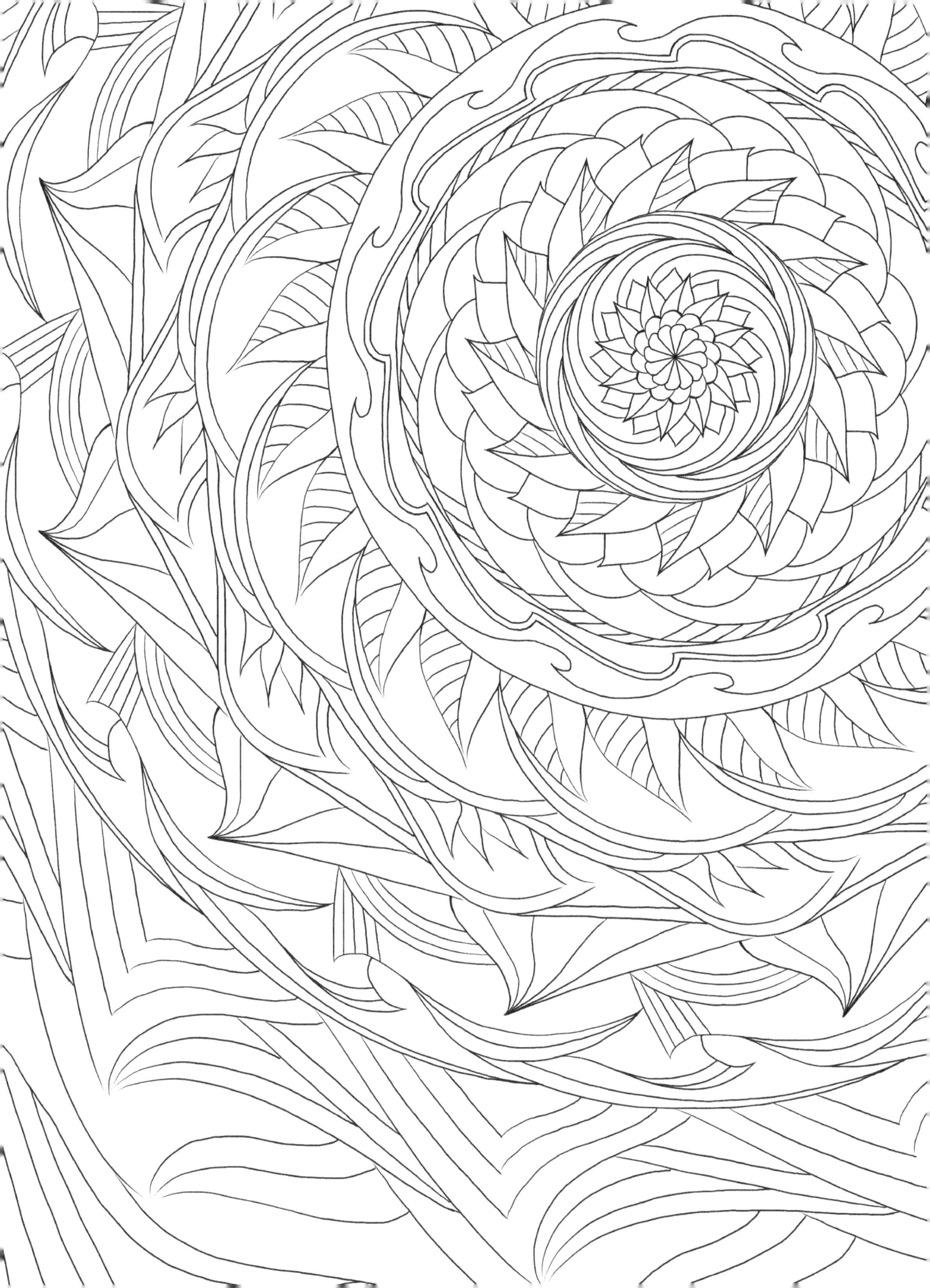

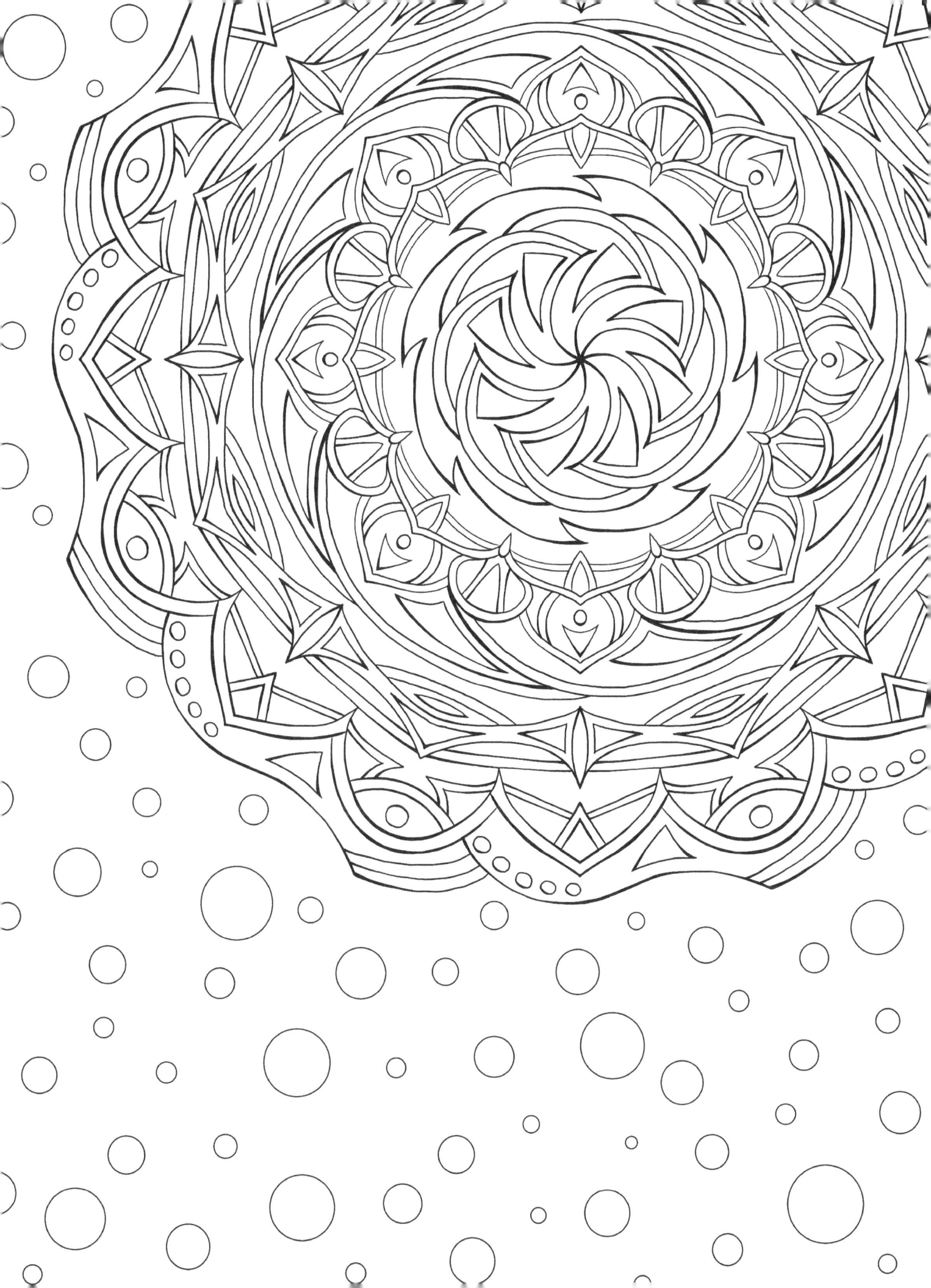

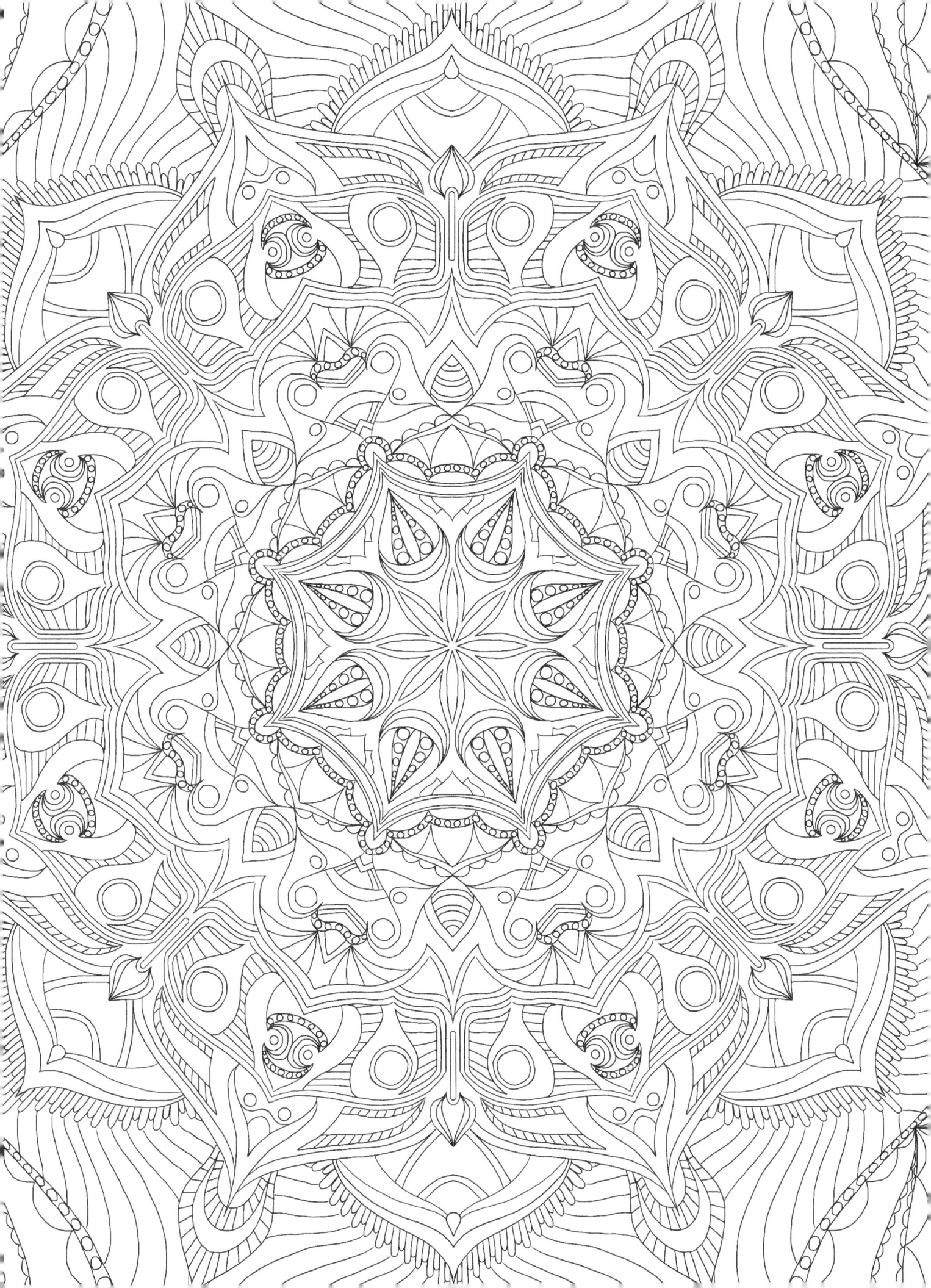

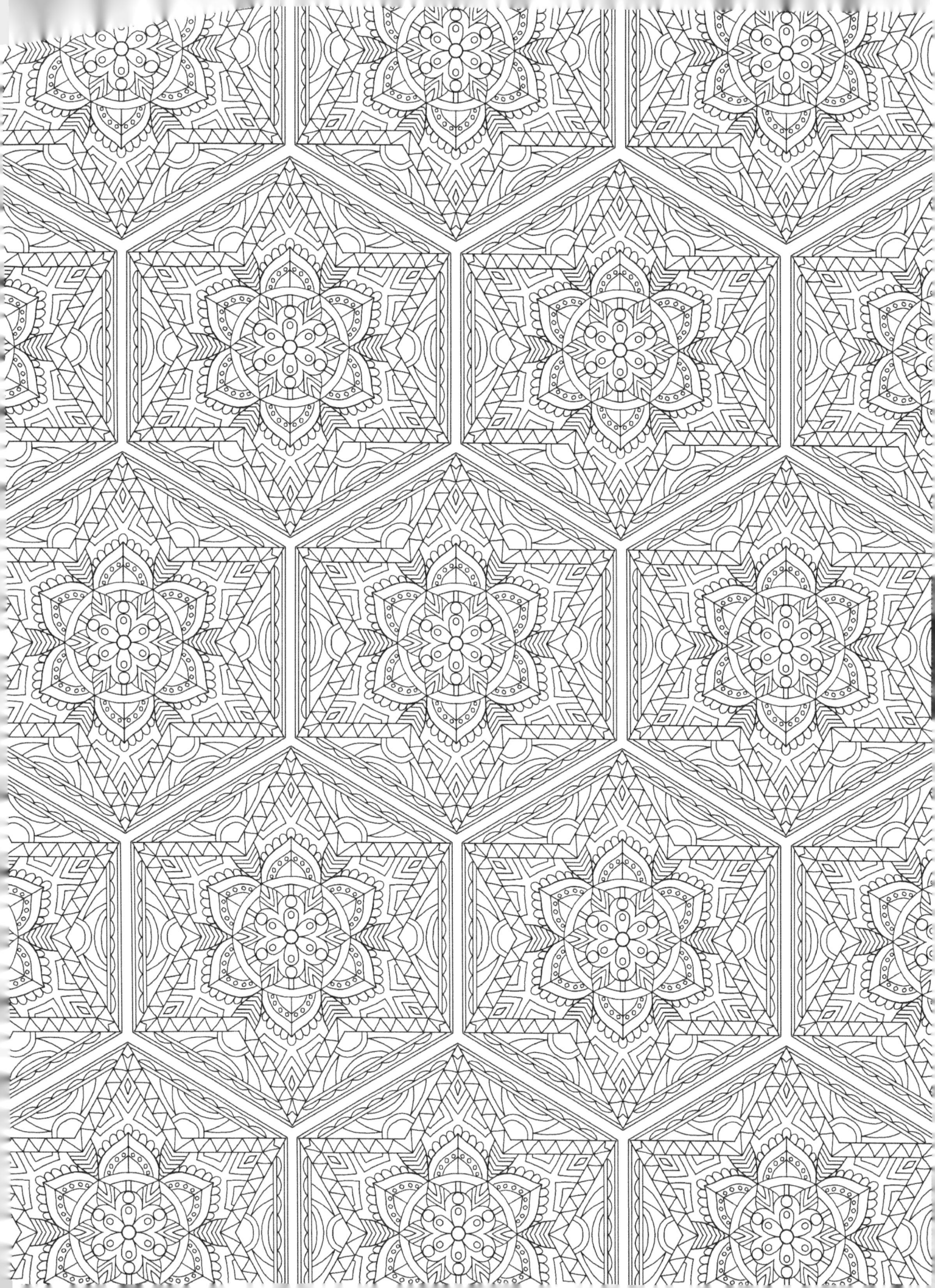

Web:

www.Lexa-Wagner.com

www.Lexa-Wagner.DeviantArt.com

Instagram: lexawagner

www.ingramcontent.com/pod-product-compliance
Lightning Source LLC
Chambersburg PA
CBHW082345220526
45470CB00008B/2642